Cloud Computing
with
Google Chrome
Volume 2

George Root

Cloud Computing with Google Chrome Volume 2

by George Root

November 2013: First Edition of Volume 2

ISBN-13:9781493744213
ISBN-10: 1493744216

Table of Contents

Preface

Introduction to the Second Volume

The first volume of this book, titled simply "**Cloud Computing with Google Chrome**", presents a lot of material primarily intended to help in understanding and setting up a new Chrome Device and is directed to readers who might not be all that familiar with the Chrome OS and how it operates. That volume presents a very good introduction to those topics and if you fall in the category of "not all that familiar with the Chrome OS and how it operates" you might like to read that volume before tackling this one.

This second volume contains all new material not presented in the first volume. Some of this new material expands upon topics introduced in the first volume and some describes entirely new topics, such as Google+, not covered at all in the first volume.

I have decided to make this new material a separate volume rather than creating a "second edition" of the original book for two reasons:

1) If I interspersed the new material throughout the original volume to create a second edition, it would be difficult for readers to identify what was new and what was original material. Readers who had already read the first volume (thank you if you fall in this category) would have had to wade through a lot of stuff they had already read in order to find the new stuff.

2) If I had created a second edition of the original book, readers who were kind enough to have purchased the original book would have had to re-buy all the old material in order to get the new stuff.

For these reasons, I have decided that the best approach is to create a separate and totally new second volume.

Just be aware, this is not a "second edition" of the original book. It does not contain any of the material presented in the original volume. You must purchase both volumes if you want to read all of the information provided.

What You Will Find in this Book

This second volume contains two types of new material:

1) Material that adds to a topic discussed in the original book. This additional information is listed here using the same Chapter and Section numbers as were in the first volume. This new material simply adds to the original sections of the book. So, for example, in "Chapter 1" in this volume, the first 5 sections, sections number 1.1 through 1.5, are missing. Those sections are contained in the original book. This "Chapter 1" starts with Section 1.6 - not contained in the original volume.

2) Entirely new material covering a topic that was not discussed in the original book is listed here with a new chapter number. These new chapters start with Chapter 12.

There is one exception to the last statement. There is a new chapter in this book, "Chapter 0", that summarizes all of the steps needed to setup and use a new Chrome Device. All of this material is presented in detail in the first volume, but I have decided to summarize it all here so that readers who may not have purchased the original volume will know what they are missing, and to act as a roadmap leading through the sometimes intricate steps need to fully set up a new Chrome Device. I have placed this new chapter, "Chapter 0", at the front of the book, so that it appears as a bridge between the first and second volumes and it also provides a baseline from which to understand what follows.

Not all of the chapters in the original volume have additional material in this second volume. So, those chapter numbers are simply missing from this volume. By looking at the Table of Contents in this volume, you should be able quickly to tell what chapters have new material and which do not.

I should again warn you that many Google services are evolving fairly rapidly with the introduction of new features and modified layouts for old features. Because of this, some things, particularly the screen shots, that you see on your computer may not be the same as what is shown in this book. Hopefully, things will remain similar enough so that you can still figure out how to use the features being described.

0 - Summary of the Steps Needed to Setup and Use Your New Chromebook

Everything you need to know to set-up your new Chromebook is described in the first volume of this book. This chapter is intended to be a brief summary of the steps needed to set-up both your Chromebook and any personal computer you want to use in conjunction with that Chromebook. For a fuller description of each step, please refer back to the first volume sections listed at the end of each step.

0.1 - Before You Start

During setup of your new Chromebook, you will have a few decisions to make and it might be a good idea to think about them before you start. The most important of these decisions are:

- Will your new Chromebook be the only computer you will use or will you want to use a personal computer in addition to your Chromebook?

- Will you want the extra security provided by Two-Step Verification?

- How will you print documents from your Chromebook?

I will expand upon each of these questions in the following paragraphs:

0.1.1 - Will You Use a Personal Computer in Addition to Your Chromebook?

It is quite possible to use a Chromebook as your only computer. But there are two downsides to this:

1) You will have to buy an ePrint enabled printer (see Section 0.1.3 below) if you want to be able to print documents from your Chromebook. If you have a personal computer with attached printers, you can use those printers to print from your Chromebook.

2) Some people find it more convenient to use a full size computer rather than the relatively small Chromebook laptop. With a personal computer you can work on the same Google Document from either your personal computer or your Chromebook.

0.1.2 - Do You Want the Extra Security Provided by Two-Step Verification?

Perhaps the biggest advantage of Chrome is security, and one key security feature of Chrome is Two-Step Verification. Briefly:

- ⊙ Without Two-Step Verification, anyone with your user name and password can access your Google Account, access your Gmail, and make purchases using Google Wallet if you have set up that feature.

- ⊙ With Two-Step Verification, nobody can access any of your Google data unless they have your user name and password and they must **also** have physical access to your cell phone. So, Two-Step Verification makes it almost impossible for someone to gain access to your Google Account, even if they have your account password. So, why wouldn't you want to enable Two-Step Verification? There is a lot of "overhead" associated with Two-Step Verification. You have to set it up. You have to generate and print "BackUp Codes". You have to generate and print "Application Specific Passwords". You have to know what "Backup Codes" and "Application Specific Passwords" are. All of this is discussed in detail in Section 3.3 of the original volume.

0.1.3 - How Do You Plan on Printing Documents from Your Chromebook?

There are three ways to print from your Chromebook:

1) Buy an ePrint (sometimes called AirPrint or iPrint or CloudPrint or ...) enabled printer. With an ePrint enabled printer, you basically send the document you want to print to the printer as an email attachment. No other computer is required. This is a good solution if your Chromebook is your only computer.

2) "Share" your existing printers that are already attached to a PC or Mac. Google CloudPrint can print to printers shared on your local network. Both the printer and your personal computer must be turned ON when you print. Your personal computer must be connected to the internet and you must have the Chrome Browser installed on your personal computer. This Chrome Browser must also be signed-in to the same Google Account as the Chromebook from which you want to print.

3) On your Chromebook, print your document to a PDF file which will be stored in your Google Drive. You will then be able to retrieve this PDF file from your Google Drive on your personal computer and print it just as you would any other file. With this option, your personal computer doesn't have to be turned ON when you print from your Chromebook. There is basically no setup required with this option, but you do need to own a personal computer with an attached printer.

How you setup printing on your Chromebook and on your personal computer depends upon which printing method you choose. Printing from your Chromebook is discussed in more detail in Chapters 5 and 6 of the original volume.

0.2 - Setting-Up Your Mac or PC

If you have a personal computer that you want to be able to access or print documents created on your Chromebook, or if you just want to use Chrome on your personal computer, there are several things you must set-up first. Here are the steps needed to set-up your personal computer:

0.2.1 - Install the Chrome Browser on Your Personal Computer

Before you can complete some of the following steps, you must download and install the free Chrome Browser on your personal computer. Get this "Chrome" at:

https://www.google.com/intl/en/chrome/browser/

0.2.2 - Create a New Google Account (Optional)

You can use the Chrome Browser on your present personal computer without setting up a Google Account. You can also use your new Chromebook without setting up a Google Account by selecting "Browse as a Guest" on the Chromebook sign-in screen. However, you cannot use any of the powerful features that Chrome provides unless you create a free Google Account. Your Google Account includes a free Gmail Account.

In order for your personal computer and your Chromebook to "work together", for example you want to print documents created on your Chromebook using a printer connected to your personal computer, then both Chromebook and your personal computer must be signed-in to the same Google Account.

If You Already Have a Google Account

Using the Chrome Browser on your personal computer, sign-in to the Google Account you will use on your Chromebook. Your personal computer must stay signed-in to this Google Account in order to be able to interact with your Chromebook.

If You Do Not Have a Google Account

Because of potential problems when trying to switch to different Google Accounts on your personal computer, I recommend that you create the Google Account that you will use on your Chromebook using your personal computer. Start by going to the Google Account sign-up page at:

https://accounts.google.com/SignUp

When you create a Google Account on your personal computer, you are automatically signed-in to that account. Although it is theoretically possible to switch to a different Google Account on your personal computer, I strongly recommend that you do not try to do it. Every time I have tried, bad things have happened.

Creating a new Google Account is discussed in Section 3.2 of the original volume.

0.2.3 - Enable Two-Step Verification for Your Google Account (Optional)

As discussed above, Two-Step Verification provides a lot of added security to your Google Account, but it also takes some extra steps to set it up.

The process of setting up Two-Step Verification is described in Section 3.3 of the original volume.

0.2.4 - Install the Google Drive App on Your PC or Mac

"Google Drive" is a block of storage space on Google's servers that is associated with your Google Account. Documents that you create on your Chromebook will be stored in your Google Drive. You can put any kind of file in your Google Drive and that file will be stored on Google's servers.

The "Google Drive App", when installed on your personal computer provides easy access to the files and documents you have stored in your Google Drive. You can download the Google Drive App for Mac, PC, iPhone/iPad, or Android device here:

https://www.google.com/intl/en_US/drive/start/download.html

When Google Drive first runs on your personal computer it asks you to sign-in to your Google Account. This links that Google Drive to that account. Any computer signed-in to that Google Account will have access to the contents of that Google Drive. So, you can put a file into your Google Drive on one computer and then take it out on another computer. This is probably the easiest way to print documents from your Chromebook.

Installing and using Google Drive is discussed in Chapter 4 of the original volume.

0.2.5 - Share Printers for Google Cloud Print

If you decided in Section 0.1.3, to print documents from your Chromebook by sending them to printers connected to your personal computer and shared on your local network, you must share those printers before you can print to them. You must also connect these shared printers to the "Google Cloud Print Connector" using your Chrome Browser.

The process of sharing printers and connecting them to the "Google Cloud Print Connector" is somewhat complicated but is fully described in Section 5.2 of the original volume.

0.2.6 - Export Your Contacts Information

If you want to transfer your "Contacts" information from your current personal computer to your Google Account, the first step is to export those contacts from your personal computer to a file that can later be imported to your Chromebook. The process for doing this is discussed in Section 9.6.2 of the original volume.

0.3 - Setting-Up Your Chromebook

Now that you have set up your personal computer to work with your Chromebook, you can start setting-up your new Chromebook.

0.3.1 - Sign-In to or Create a Google Account (Optional)

If you plan to keep your current personal computer so that it can interact with your Chromebook, for example by printing documents created on your Chromebook, then I recommend that you have already created the Google Account you will use on both your personal computer and your Chromebook using your personal computer as described above in Section 0.2.2 .

If You Already Have a Google Account

On the Sign-In screen simply enter the user name and password for the primary Google Account you will use on both Chromebook and personal computer. Remember that the first user to sign-in on a new Chromebook becomes the "owner" of that Chromebook. The "owner" of the Chromebook has privileges that other users do not. If you have enabled Two-Step Verification when you created your account, you will be asked to enter a 6-digit code that will be sent to you on your cell phone.

If You Do Not Have a Google Account

If the Chromebook is your only computer, or if you never plan to interact with any other personal computer you may own, then you can create a new Google Account directly on your Chromebook.

Start by clicking "Create a Google Account" on the right side of the Chromebook sign-in screen. If you create a new account on a new Chromebook, that user account becomes the "owner" of that Chromebook. The "owner" of the Chromebook has privileges that other users do not.

Creating a new Google Account is discussed in Section 3.2 of the original volume.

0.3.2 - Edit Your Google Account Settings

This would be a good time to adjust some of your Account Settings. These might also be called user preferences. They are specific to this particular Chromebook. Some of these settings impact the security of your Chromebook.

You can access your Google Account Settings in either of two ways:

1) Click on the "Chrome Menu" icon. It looks like three horizontal bars in the upper-right corner of the Chrome Browser window and select "Settings"

2) Click on the photo associated with your account in the lower-right corner of the Chromebook Browser window and select "Settings"

There are several settings you can choose but I will only discuss a few of them here. A more complete listing is given in Section 3.7 of the original volume. All of the settings are pretty self explanatory. Here are the ones I think are most important:

- **Adjust Touchpad Settings**: Settings > Device > Touchpad Settings. I like to enable "Tap-to-Click" (tapping once on the Touchpad is equivalent to clicking the left button on a mouse), but you may not. You can also decide which direction you prefer for scrolling.

- **Turn on Encryption**: Settings > Users > Advanced Sync Settings > Encrypt All Data (Recommended). See Section 3.3.1 of the original volume for a more complete description.

- **Enable or Disable Guest Browsing**: Settings > Users > Manage Other Users > Disable Guest Browsing (Recommended). If you enable Guest Browsing, a thief could use your Chromebook even without your sign-in credentials. So, unless you have a specific reason to want to allow someone else to use your Chromebook without signing-in to your Google Account, there is no point in leaving Guest Browsing Enabled.

- **Restrict Other Users**: Settings > Users > Manage Other Users > Restrict Sign-In to the Following Users (Recommended). This restricts the Google Accounts that can sign-in on your device. By restricting possible sign-ins to a specific list that you create, a thief would not be able to use your stolen Chromebook to sign-in to his or her own account. Once again, unless you have some reason to do otherwise, I recommend setting this restriction and entering a list of user accounts that you want to allow to use your device. If you are the only user of your Chromebook, you can limit users to just your own account.

- **Passwords and Forms**: Settings > Show Advanced Settings > Passwords and Forms. Having Chrome remember your form fill and password information is very convenient, but it is also a security risk. If Chrome automatically fills in your passwords for you, it is pretty much as if you didn't have a password. Personally, I disable both AutoFill and "Save My Passwords" in my Chrome Settings and then I use a separate password manager, with a different password, to accomplish those things. I use "LastPass" which is an excellent password and form fill Chrome Extension (download it from the Chrome Web Store - see Section 2.7 of the original volume). LastPass is another cloud based application. LastPass runs on every available computer and mobile device and, because it is cloud based, all of your passwords and form-fill data are available on any device you have installed LastPass on. All of the encryption and decryption takes place on your device and no unencrypted data leaves your device. The folks at LastPass do not have access to your LastPass password, so only you can decrypt your sensitive information.

- **Google Cloud Print**: Settings > Show Advanced Settings > Google Cloud Print > Sign-In to Google Cloud Print. If you have opted to use an ePrint enabled printer with your Chromebook, you can skip this step. If you have decided to print from your Chromebook by first printing to a PDF file on your Chromebook and then printing that PDF file using your personal computer, then you can also skip this step.

  OK, if you have arrived here, that means that you intend to print from your Chromebook using a printer attached to your personal computer, Mac, PC, or Linux, and shared with your Chromebook over your local network. At this point, you should have already shared your printer(s) on your personal computer as described in Section 0.2.5. If you have not, go back and do it now - I'll wait.

When you click on "Settings > Show Advanced Settings > Google Cloud Print" the first time, you will be asked to sign-in to your Google Account. This must be the same account you were signed-in to on your personal computer when you shared your printer(s) and set-up Google Cloud Print Connector. It must also be the Google Account you are currently using on your Chromebook. After this first time, the "Google Cloud Print" setting will say "Open Google Cloud Print" or "Manage Google Cloud Print".

At this point you should see a list of the printers you have shared from your personal computer. Select the printers you will want to use from your Chromebook and click on "Add Printers". Now, when you "Print" anything on your Chromebook, you should see a list of the printers you have selected and you can choose which one you want to use to print the current file.

Setting Up and Using Google Cloud Print is described in Chapters 5 and 6 of the original volume.

0.3.3 - Edit Your Google Account Security Settings

These settings apply to any device signed-in to your Google Account. You may have already set up your account security settings when you created your Google Account. If not, start setting them up by going here:

https://www.google.com/settings/security

The page that opens has five categories of settings that you can make or modify:

- **Password**: This is where you can change your account password

- **Recovery Options**: Be sure to supply a phone number and an email address that is different from your Gmail address. If you ever forget your account password, this is how Google will help you recover your account data so provide good information here. You may need it one day.

- **Notifications**: If you want to be notified of suspicious account activity, provide a valid email address and phone number. This can be your Gmail address.

- **2-Step Verification**: This is a biggie. If you leave 2-Step turned OFF, your account will be protected only by your user name and password. If you turn it ON, someone trying to sign-on to your account - think a hacker somewhere in Russia - will also need to have physical access to your cell phone. So, 2-Step provides a lot of extra security, but it does take a fair amount of set-up and maintenance. Read Sections 3.3.2 and 3.3.3 of the original volume for the full story.

- **Connected Applications and Sites**: You will be asked to sign-in to your account again to verify that you are you. Here you will find a listing, some might say a frightening listing, of all the apps and extensions you have installed in your Google Account and the access those entities have to your account information. For example, here you will find that Gmail for iOS devices has full access to all of your account data. You can revoke these access privileges, but then the associated app or extension may (will) not work. You can read more about access permissions in Section 2.7.5 of the original volume.

This Account Security Settings page also provides the ability to generate and print Application Specific Passwords. These are part of 2-Step Verification. You can read more about all this in Section 3.3 of the original volume.

0.3.4 - Edit Your Google Mail Settings

While we are editing settings, we might as well finish up by taking a look at your Gmail settings. You can access these settings by opening Gmail and clicking on the "Gear" icon near the upper right corner of the Gmail window and clicking on the "Settings" item in the drop down menu that appears. There are literally hundreds of settings that control how Gmail looks and operates. I will only discuss a few of the important ones here. You can read a little more about Gmail settings in Sections 9.3 and 9.4 of the original volume.

Note: If you change any of the following Gmail Settings, be sure to click on the "Save Changes" button at the bottom of the window.

Settings Under the "General" Tab:

- ◉ **External Content:** Settings > General > External Content. I recommend selecting "Ask Before Displaying External Content". In the past "External Content", such as images, have been used as infection vectors. Many "external content" images are just advertising and waste bandwidth to display. So, my default is not to display external content unless I approve it.

- ◉ **Desktop Notifications:** Settings > General > Desktop Notifications. I turn "New Mail Notification" ON. When a new email arrives, my iPhone beeps and lets me read the first line of the message without entering my security code. This works well for me mainly because I don't receive much email. If you receive hundreds of messages a day, this might be pretty annoying and you might opt to turn notifications OFF.

- ◉ **Signature:** Settings > General > Signature. You can set-up a default signature that will be appended to the end of all your outgoing Gmail messages.

Settings Under the "Inbox" Tab:

- ◉ **Inbox Type:** Settings > Inbox > Inbox Type. There are 4 or 5 possible arrangements of messages in your Inbox. I like the "Unread First" style. This puts all of my unread messages in a chronological list at the top of my Inbox. Once I read a message, it gets demoted down to another chronological list of all my read messages. Choose a style that appeals to you.

Settings Under the "Accounts" Tab:

- **Send Mail As:** Settings > Accounts > Send Mail As: The default is to send messages from your Gmail account, but if you own other email accounts, you can select to have your outgoing messages appear to have been sent from one of the other accounts that you own.

- **Check Mail from Other Accounts**: Settings > Accounts > Check Mail from Other Accounts > Add a POP3 Mail Account You Own. This a very powerful feature. Gmail can collect email messages sent to any of the other (up to five) email accounts you may own provided that those other accounts support POP3 access. Just click on the "Add a POP3 Mail Account You Own" button and follow the instructions. You can also apply a label to this type of message so that you can tell which account it was actually sent to. Refer to Section 9.4.3 of the original volume for more information.

- **Add Additional Storage**: Settings > Accounts > Add Additional Storage. This is where you can buy additional storage on Google servers. This includes Google Drive storage, not just Gmail storage.

Settings Under the "Labs" Tab:

Gmail "Labs" provides extensions to standard Gmail that may enhance its functionality. Or it might not. "Labs" are sort of experimental and some may not work entirely. But you can try any of them and see if you like them. Here are a few that you might find useful:

- **Mark as Read Button:** Marks the current message as "Read" without having to go thru a menu.

- **Quote Selected Text**: Select some text in a message and then, when you reply to that message, the selected text is "quoted" in the reply.

- **Undo Send**: Allows you to cancel sending a message for a few seconds after you hit the "Send" button.

There are a lot of other things under the "Labs" menu and they change from time to time, so check it out.

Settings Under the "Offline" Tab:

"Gmail Offline" allows you to read and compose messages even when you are offline. Messages you send will not actually be sent until you are back online. Similarly, you will not be able to see any messages that arrive after you go offline, but they will appear when you go back online again.

- **Install Gmail Offline:** Clicking on this button will take you to the Chrome Web Store where you can install the Gmail Offline app. Click on the "Launch App" button and that will take you to a screen where you can Enable offline reading and replying to messages. Be aware however that the way this works is to download your Gmail messages to the computer you are using at the time. So, do not enable this app if you sometimes use a public computer.

"Account Activity" - Available in Any Tab:

While we are discussing Gmail Settings, there is a potentially very useful feature of Gmail hidden at the bottom of all of the Gmail Settings Tabs. Scroll down to the bottom of any Tab window and along the right edge of the window is a button labeled "Open in # Other Locations Details" where "#" is the number of other computers that are currently signed-in to your Gmail account. Clicking on the "Details" button will provide you with a listing of all computers currently signed-in along with a history of recent Gmail account activity. A potentially very useful button is located at the top of this window. It is labeled "Sign-Out of All Other Sessions". This might be useful if you were using an Internet Cafe computer and forgot to sign-out of your Gmail session. Or, more sinister, it could allow you to terminate the session opened by that hacker in China that has been reading your email.

0.3.5 - Edit Your Google Drive Settings

Launch the Google Drive app on your Chromebook and click on the "Gear" icon in the upper right corner. This will open a window with a menu of settings you can adjust to your preference. The most important of these are:

"Upload Settings" Under the Google Drive "Gear" Icon:

When you move a file from your personal computer to the Google Drive folder, you are actually "uploading" that file to the Google servers. If the file you are uploading is an "Office" file, i.e. a Word, Excel, or PowerPoint file, you can store those files in your Google Drive, but you cannot edit those files directly in Google Drive because Google does not (yet) have apps that can edit "Office" files directly. Google Drive can display Office files, but it cannot edit them in their native format. But, you can convert these file types into native Google Documents that you can edit in Google Drive. A Word file would be converted into a Google Doc file. An Excel file would be converted into a Google Sheets file. And a PowerPoint file would be converted into a Google Slides file. This menu item, "Upload Settings" allows you to choose how you want Google to handle this type of file. There are three of these settings:

- ◉ **"Convert Uploaded Files to Google Docs Format":** If you click on this setting, all "Office" file types will always be converted to Google Docs files when they are uploaded to your Google Drive.

- ◉ **"Convert Text from Uploaded PDF and Image Files":** If you select this setting and upload a PDF or image file that contains text, Google will perform Optical Character Recognition (OCR) on that file and produce an editable text document.

- ◉ **"Confirm Settings Before Each Upload":** With this setting enabled, each time you start to upload a file to your Google Drive of a type that can be converted, you will be asked to confirm how you want that file handled.

"Manage Apps" Settings Under the Google Drive "Gear" Icon:

Google Drive is not just a file repository. It also hosts a set of apps that can operate on those file. For example, there is a "Google Docs" app that allows you to create or edit Google Docs documents. These include word processing documents (Google Docs - see Section 7.4 of the original volume), spreadsheet documents (Google Sheets - see Section 7.5 of the original volume), and slide presentation documents (Google Slides - see Section 7.5 of the original volume). There is an app that allows you to create and edit Google Drawings - see Section 7.6 of the original volume. There is another that lets you create and edit Google Forms - see Section 7.7 of the original volume.

The "Manage Apps" menu item under the Google Drive "Gear" icon lets you install and manage these and other Google Drive apps. You can learn more about all this by clicking on the "Learn More" button at the top of the "Manage Apps" window.

0.3.6 - Enable Offline Access

Since we have been talking about Google Drive and Google Apps, this would be a good time to enable offline access if you want to do that. Normally, all of your files are stored on Google servers and are therefore not available to you unless you are connected to the Internet. However, if you enable offline access, Chrome installs apps on your Chromebook that allow you to create and edit Google Docs files. With offline access enabled, some of your recent Google Docs files are also downloaded to your Chromebook so that you can view and/or edit them.

To enable offline access, refer to Section 7.1 of the original volume which provides a fairly complete description of the process.

0.3.7 - Import Your Contacts Information

If you have exported your Contacts information from your personal computer, you can now import them into the Google Contacts app. The process for doing this is described in Section 9.6.2 of the original volume.

0.3.8 - Install More Apps and Extensions

Now that you have your Chromebook all set up and ready to use, you might want to visit the Chrome Web Store and install more apps and extensions. The process for doing this is described in Section 2.7 of the original volume.

On the next page are a few apps and extensions that you might find useful. Check them out at the Chrome Web Store. If you have enabled offline access, you can find a collection of apps that can be used without an Internet connection. In the Chrome Web Store go to Apps > Collections > Offline to find both Google as well as 3rd party apps that work offline.

- **"LastPass"**
- **"EverNote"**
- **"Feedly"**
- **"Kindle Cloud Reader"**
- **"The Weather Channel"**
- **"Clearly"**
- **"AdBlock"**
- **"iCloud"**
- **"Print Friendly & PDF"**
- **"Send this Link with Gmail"**
- **"Google Voice"**

1 - What is Google Chrome?

1.6 - Updating Google Chrome

Here's what Google says about updating Chrome: "Google Chrome automatically updates whenever it detects that a new version of the browser is available. The update process happens in the background and doesn't require any action on your part." But then Google goes on to describe how you perform the update process. So, some minimal action on your part is sometimes required.

Some updates to Chrome can occur entirely in the background without any intervention on your part. But other updates require that your Chrome device be restarted in order for the update process to be completed. Google cannot, or at least chooses not to, restart your Chrome device without your permission. So, they send you a subtle message that a restart is required and then they wait patiently for you to do that.

1.6.1 - Updating Chrome OS on Your Samsung (or Other) Chromebook

When an update to the Chrome OS that requires a restart is available on the Samsung Chromebook (and I presume on other Chrome Devices), a new icon appears in the "Status" area of the "Launcher and Status Bar" at the bottom right corner of the screen as illustrated in Figure 1.1. It looks like an upward pointing arrow as is shown next to the 10:15 time in Figure 1.1.

Figure 1.1 The Upward Pointing Arrow Icon Indicates that an Update to Chrome OS that Requires a Restart is Available

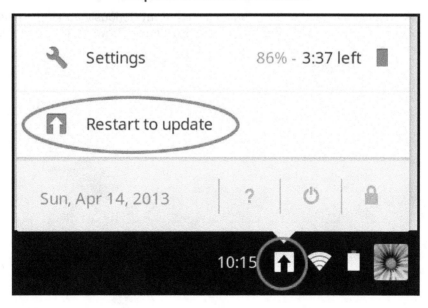

If you hover the cursor over this upward pointing arrow icon, the message "Update Available" will appear. Clicking on the icon itself will initiate the OS update process by displaying the message "Restart to update" as illustrated in Figure 1.1. Clicking on "Restart to update" will install the updated Chrome OS and restart your Chromebook.

1.6.2 - Updating the Chrome Browser on Your personal computer

Here's what Google says about an "automatic" update to the Chrome Browser: "Updates are available if the Chrome menu on the browser toolbar shows a little arrow . To apply the update, just follow the steps below.

- Click the Chrome menu on the browser toolbar.

- Select Update Google Chrome.

- In the confirmation dialog that appears, click 'Restart'. The browser saves your opened tabs and windows and reopens them automatically when it restarts. If you'd prefer not to restart right away, click 'Not now'. The next time you restart your browser, the update will automatically be applied."

1.6.3 - Manually Checking for Updates to the Chrome Browser

Here's what Google says about checking to see if your Chrome Browser is up to date:

"Click the Chrome menu on the browser toolbar, or type alt+e on your Chromebook to reveal the Chrome Menu, and select 'About Google Chrome'. The current version number is the series of numbers beneath the "Google Chrome" heading. Chrome will check for updates when you're on this page. Click Relaunch to apply any available update."

So, keep a lookout for an upward pointing arrow icon that mysteriously appears in the status area of your Chromebook or in the Chrome menu icon in your Chrome Browser. If you see one of these up-arrows, click on it.

2 - Getting Familiar with Your Chrome Device

2.1.2 - Chrome Keyboard Shortcuts

There are many keyboard shortcuts that you can use with your Chromebook. I presented a short list of some of the more useful ones in the original Section 2.1.2. But, there is an easier way to see all of the keyboard shortcuts available on your Chrome Device. Just hold down the "ctrl" and the "alt" keys and type a backslash "/". This will display a view of your keyboard with all of the shortcuts labeled on their respective keys as is illustrated in Figure 2.14.

Figure 2.14 Typing ctrl+alt+/ Reveals a Map of All Available Keyboard Shortcuts

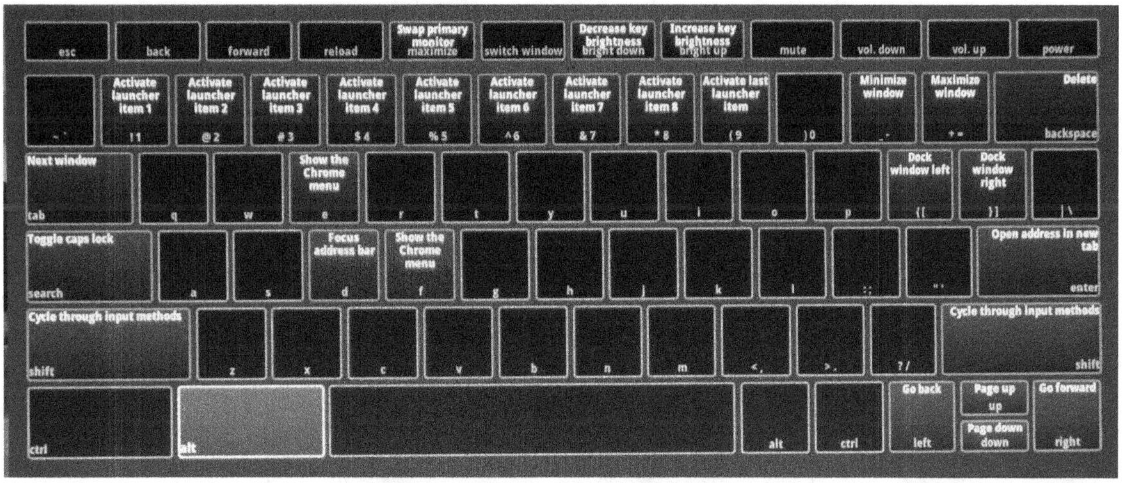

Figure 2.14 shows all of the keyboard shortcuts available on my Samsung Chromebook when holding down the "alt" key. You can see other shortcuts by holding down the ctrl, the alt, and the shift keys in their various combinations. To exit this keyboard view, you can type ctrl+alt+/ again, or even easier, just hit "esc" in the upper-left corner of the keyboard. Different Chrome Devices may have different keyboard shortcuts and all of them may not be implemented by the Chrome Device manufacturer.

2.3.4 - The Google "Black Bar" - Update

The Google "Black Bar", which was described in this section of the original volume has been (mostly) replaced by a new icon that provides immediate access to Google services from any browser window.

This new "waffle icon" appears near the upper-right corner of the Chrome Browser window running on your personal computer as illustrated in Figure 2.15.

Figure 2.15 - The New Google Services Icon in the Chrome Browser

Clicking on the "Waffle Icon" circled in the figure opens the drop-down array of icons representing some of the more popular Google Services. If the service you are looking for is not in this array, clicking on the "More" button at the bottom of the array will open a complete list of all Google Services.

If you like the old "new tab" window that showed an array of all the apps installed in your Chrome Browser, you can still access that. The icon that opens this apps window is in the upper-left corner of the browser window as shown in Figure 2.16. If you are using a Chromebook, this apps waffle icon appears at the right end of the Launcher and Status bar at the bottom of the browser window as described in section 2.4 of the original volume.

Figure 2.16 - The New Google Services Icon in the Chrome Browser

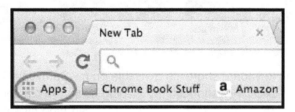

2.3.7 - Syncing Browser Tabs

Suppose that you are reading a web page using the Chrome Browser on your PC at work. But you don't have time to finish reading it before leaving for home. Later, that evening, you open your Chromebook and want to finish reading the page. But you can't remember the page address (URL). You could have emailed the page URL to yourself before closing down at work, but Chrome provides a much easier way to solve this problem.

Google keeps track of all the Tabs you have open on all of your devices. So, you can open a Tab that you had open on your work PC, from your Chromebook at home. This is called "Tab Syncing". You do need to set up Tab Syncing on all the devices you want to stay in sync before you can use this feature. All the devices you want to stay in sync must be signed-in to the same Google Account.

Setting Up Tab Syncing on Windows, Mac, Linux, or Chrome Devices

- Open the Chrome Browser Menu by clicking on the icon at the far right end of the Chrome Browser Tab Bar that looks like three horizontal bars (see Figure 2.3) and select "Settings". On the Mac this can also be accomplished by holding down the "command" key and typing a comma.

- In the Settings window that opens, find the "Advanced Sync Settings" button. This will be in a different location depending upon whether you are using the Chrome Browser (see Figure 2.17) or a Chromebook (see Figure 2.18).

- Clicking on the "Advanced Sync Settings" button will open a window as shown in Figure 2.18.

- If you want the Open Tabs on this device to be synced with your other devices, then be sure the checkbox next to "Open Tabs" is checked as shown in Figure 2.19. If you don't want the tabs on this device to be synced with your other devices, make sure this checkbox is not checked. For example, you may not want tabs on your home computer to be synced with your work computer.

Figure 2.17 - The Advanced Sync Settings Button in the Chrome Browser

Figure 2.18 - The Advanced Sync Settings Button on a Chromebook

Figure 2.19 - The Advanced Sync Settings Window

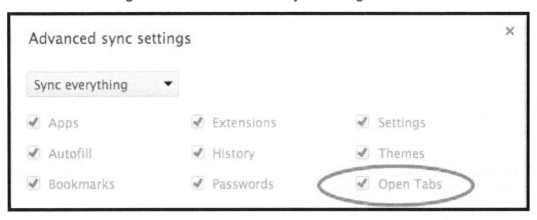

While you're here in this window, you might want to check or uncheck the other items that Chrome will sync across your devices.

Setting Up Tab Syncing on iOS Devices

- Open the Chrome Browser and touch the Chrome Menu Icon. This is the icon that looks like three horizontal bars at the upper right corner of the browser window. You may have to scroll the window down so that you can see the upper corner.

- Scroll down in the list that opens and touch "Settings"

- Touch your email address

- Under the "Services" label, make sure that "Sync" is turned on and then touch "Advanced".

- If you want to sync everything, including your Open Tabs, just be sure that the "Sync Everything" switch is turned "ON". If you want to choose which items to sync and which to not sync, turn the "Sync Everything" switch "OFF".

- If you have turned "Sync Everything" to "OFF", a list of items that can be synced will open. Just turn items that you want to keep in sync to "ON" and those you don't want to sync to "OFF".

- Touch "Done" and you're done. Your Open Tabs and other things that you have turned "ON" will now stay in sync on this device.

Setting Up Tab Syncing on Android Devices

I don't own an Android device, so I will just repeat what Google says about tab syncing on Android devices:

- Touch Chrome Menu > "Settings" > your email address

- Touch "Sync" and make sure the "Open tabs" checkbox is selected if you want to sync your open tabs on this device or is not selected if you do not want your tabs on this device to be synced.

Opening Tabs from Another Device

Now that you have set up tab syncing, you can make use of this magical service. Suppose that you are at home and you want to continue reading that article that you were reading while using Chrome at work. Just open a New Tab (see Figure 2.3). In the upper right corner of the New Tab window, click on the Chrome Menu icon - it looks like three horizontal bars as illustrated in the upper-left corner of Figure 2.20. This will drop down a menu - click on the "Recent Tabs" item. This opens a list of items also shown in Figure 2.20.

Figure 2.20 - Selecting the "Recent Tabs" Button Reveals a Long List of Items

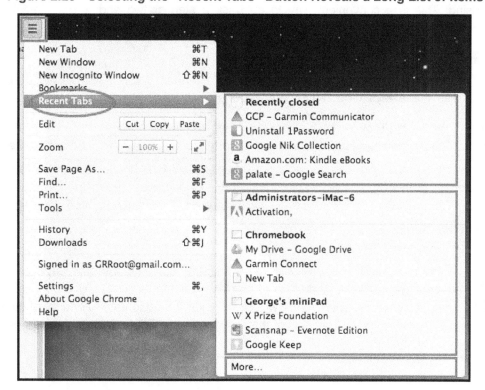

Clicking on the "Recent Tabs" button illustrated in Figure 2.20 will reveal a list of items as shown in the figure. This list has three main parts.

- ⦿ "Recently Closed" - This is the first item outlined at the top of the list. It contains a list of tabs that were recently closed on the device you are using. So you can go back to a recently closed tab by clicking on the desired tab in this list.

- ⦿ "Open Tabs on Other Devices" - This section contains a list of your other synced devices and the open tabs on those devices. In Figure 2.20 there is no label "Open Tabs on Other Devices". Instead there is simply a list of other devices and the tabs that are currently open on those devices. So, in Figure 2.20, the items "Administrators-iMac-6", "Chromebook", and "George's miniPad" are my three other synced devices and the list of open tabs on those devices. These other devices don't have to be running - Google knows what tabs were open when they were running. You can simply click on any of the tabs listed and that webpage will open in your current Chrome Browser window.

⦿ The last item, at the bottom of the list, is "More ...". Clicking on "More ..." will open a separate window with a full list of your browsing history. This is described in the next section.

2.3.8 - Accessing and Clearing Your Browser History

Short Term Memory

The "Recent Tabs" menu item illustrated in Figure 2.20 provides a short term memory of your browsing history. Clicking on this button reveals a list of "Recently Closed" tabs on the device you are currently using. This is a convenient way to go back a step or two and re-open a tab that you inadvertently closed.

Long Term Memory

There are at least three ways to open a full list of your browsing history:

1) Go to the Chrome Browser Menu (that three bar icon in the upper right corner of the browser window) and select the "History" item about two-thirds of the way to the bottom of the menu

2) On a Chromebook, you can access your browser history by holding down the "ctrl" key and typing "h". In the Chrome Browser running on my iMac, I can open the History window by typing "Command" + "Y". I'm sure there will be keyboard shortcuts on other devices.

3) Go to the Chrome Browser Menu (that three bar icon in the upper right corner of the browser window) and select "Recent Tabs" -> "More ...". The "More ..." item is at the bottom of the list.

Doing any of these things will reveal a list of open tabs on your other Chrome devices and a long history of your browsing on your current device arranged chronologically by date and time. This history will go back about a month and there will be an "Older ..." button at the bottom of the list if you need to see even older history. The top part of this list is shown in Figure 2.21 on the next page.

Clearing Your Browsing History

To erase all or part of your browsing history, open the browsing history window using any of the techniques described in the previous section. The top portion of the history window that opens is shown in Figure 2.21. Near the top of this window there is a button labelled "Clear Browsing Data ...". This button is outlined in Figure 2.21. Clicking this button will open a window as illustrated in Figure 2.22. Just select the items you wish to delete and click on the "Clear Browsing Data" button in the lower-right corner of the window.

Figure 2.21 - The Browser History Window Contains a "Clear Browsing Data" Button

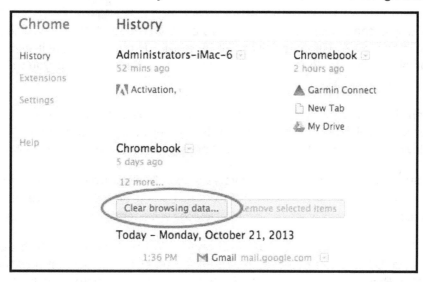

Figure 2.22 - You Can Clear Your Browsing History in This Window

2.8 - Using External Devices with Your Chromebook

Chromebooks are pretty well equipped but sometimes it might be desirable to add functionality by attaching an external device, such as a hard drive or external monitor. This section briefly describes a few of the possible external devices you might want to attach to your Chromebook.

2.8.1 - Using an External Drive with Your Chromebook

Most Chrome Devices come equipped with either 16 or 32 GB Solid State Drives. The Acer C7 is an exception since it has a 320 GB hard drive built in. But in general, and specifically if you have a Samsung Chromebook, in order to store a lot of "stuff" on your Chrome Device, you will have to resort to external storage of some sort.

For modest quantities of "stuff" - an additional 16 or 32 GB for example - you can insert an SD Card in the card reader slot provided with ChromeBooks. For larger quantities of storage, you can use an external hard drive connect through one of the USB ports provided on your ChromeBook.

The exact procedure for using an external drive with your Chrome Device will depend upon which Chrome Device you have. In this section I will discuss using an external drive with a Samsung Chromebook. I expect that other types of Chrome Devices will operate in a similar manner.

The Samsung Chromebook has one USB 2 and one USB 3 port, either of which can be used to connect an external USB drive to your ChromeBook. In order to find out just how this operates, I purchased a LaCie Porsche Design 500 GB USB 3.0 Mobile Drive - approximately $80 at Amazon. I chose this drive because it can be formatted for either Windows or Mac OS X file formats. As it turned out, formatting the drive as Windows FAT 32 worked well and there was no need for the MAC OS X (HFS+) file support.

Formatting an External Drive

Right out of the box, the LaCie mobile drive is not recognized by the ChromeBook. The drive comes with formatting software that runs on Windows and Mac OS X computers, but not on Chrome computers. So, before you can use an external drive with your ChromeBook, you will first have to connect the drive to either a Windows or Mac computer. I used my iMac which can format drives in either Mac OS X (HFS+) or Windows (FAT32) formats. If you buy a "Windows Only" drive, you will be able to format it as a FAT 32 drive on your Windows personal computer and that should work fine.

When I ran the LaCie drive formatting app on my Mac, I had the choice of dividing the drive into two partitions, one formatted for Windows (FAT32) and the other formatted for Mac OS X (HFS+). Because, at this point, I didn't know which format would work, I chose to divide the drive into two equal sized partitions with one formatted as FAT32 and the other formatted as HFS+ as illustrated in Figure 2.23. After formatting, these two "drives" showed up on my Desktop with names "LACIE SHARE" for the FAT32 partition and "LaCie" for the HFS+ partition as illustrated in Figure 2.24. At this point I could have renamed the partitions "FAT32" and "HFS+", or anything else.

If you have a drive that has already been formatted as a FAT32 volume, you can reformat it directly on the ChromeBook. Simply right-click on the name of the drive in the Chrome File System window (see Figure 4.3), and select "Format". This will erase everything on the drive and prepare it for use with your ChromeBook. This drive will be named UNTITLED and that cannot be changed.

Figure 2.23 - Formatting the External Drive into Two Partitions

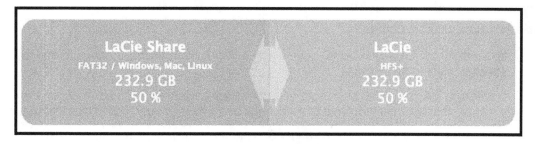

Figure 2.24 - After Formatting, the External Drive Appears as Two Separate Volumes

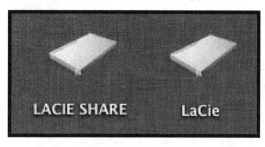

Chrome OS recognizes several other file systems, but FAT32 and NTFS are the most likely to support read/write on a Chrome Device. Chrome recognizes HFS+ files written by Mac OS X, but they are read-only. So you could write files to an HFS+ formatted drive on your Mac and then read those files on your ChromeDevice, but you cannot write files to an HFS+ formatted drive from Chrome.

Using an External Drive

After formatting the external drive, I plugged it back into my ChromeBook USB 3 port. Both partitions were recognized immediately as illustrated in Figure 2.25.

Figure 2.25 - Both Formatted Volumes Are Recognized by the Chrome File System

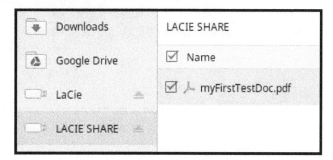

I wrote the file "myFirstTestDoc.pdf" to the "LACIE SHARE" (FAT32) drive on my ChromeBook by dragging it from my Google Drive folder onto the "LACIE SHARE" drive illustrated in Figure 2.25. However, when I tried the same thing with the "LaCie" (HFS+) drive, it failed to copy proving that, at least at this time, HFS+ formatted drives are recognized as read-only when attached to ChromeBooks.

Conclusions About Using Your External Drive

The conclusions of this exercise are:

- You must format a new external drive using a Windows or Mac OS computer before you can attach it to your ChromeBook.

- Formatting it as a FAT32 drive using your Windows or Macintosh personal computer will result in a drive that will mount on your Chromebook and which you can use to read or write files.

- If you format the external drive as an HFS+ volume, it will mount, but will be read-only.

Figure 2.26 - My Samsung Chromebook with 500 GB of External Storage

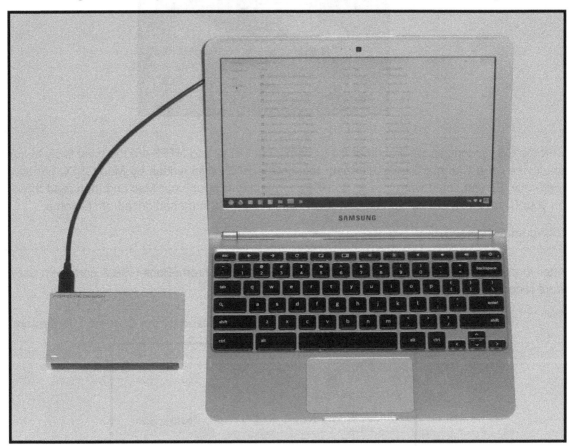

2.8.2 - Using Ethernet with Your Samsung Chromebook

Samsung Chromebooks, Google "Pixels", and some other Chrome Devices do not come with Ethernet ports. They rely on wireless, WiFi or cellular data to connect to the internet. But, what about those situations where there is no WiFi? Some hotels offer Ethernet connections, but not WiFi. This is bad news, particularly if your Chrome Device doesn't have cell data capability. Fortunately, there is an excellent USB to Ethernet adaptor that allows your Chromebook to connect to the internet with a wired connection. Not only is this type of connection more secure than WiFi, it is also faster.

I have only tested one Ethernet adaptor for my Chromebook, and it works perfectly. I can recommend it if you want to cover all of your bases with respect to Internet connectivity. The adaptor I have tested is the "Plugable USB 2.0 to 10/100/1000 Gigabit Ethernet Wired Network Adapter for Windows, Mac, Chromebook, and Linux". I bought mine from Amazon for $25. If your "other computer" is a MacBook "Air", this adaptor will also work with that laptop. However, you will have to install a driver if you are using this adaptor with a Mac or Windows personal computer. Chrome devices don't require a driver.

Connecting Your Chromebook to the Internet via Ethernet

The "Plugable" USB to Ethernet adaptor works with the Samsung Chromebook right out of the box. It is not necessary to install a driver since Chrome devices come with one built-in. Ethernet cables are not "hot swappable" meaning that they should not be connected nor disconnected when power is applied. Here is the sequence I used to connect my Chromebook to the Ethernet:

- Close the cover of the Chromebook so that power to the USB ports is turned off.
- Plug the Ethernet cable into the "Plugable" adaptor
- Plug the "Plugable" adaptor into one of the USB ports on the Chromebook
- Open the cover.

If you watch the lower right corner of the Chromebook screen, in the "Status Area", when you open the cover, you will see that the icon representing a WiFi connection disappears and is replaced with … nothing. But, if you click on your Account photo to open the Settings window, you will see that your Chromebook is "Connected to Ethernet" as shown in Figure 2.27. That's all there is to connecting your Chromebook to Ethernet.

Figure 2.27 The Ethernet Connection is Recognized Automatically

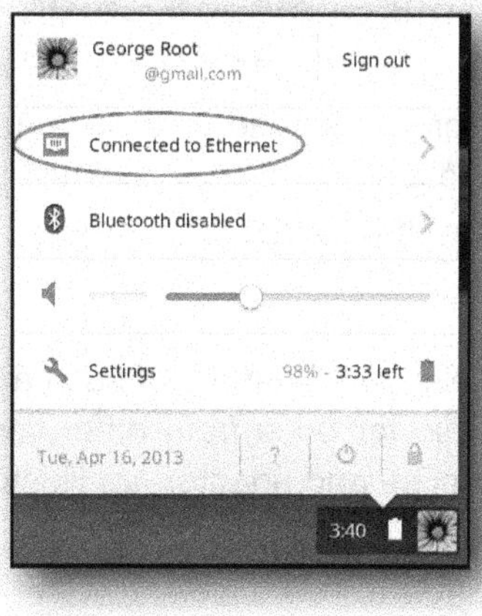

Disconnecting Your Chromebook from Ethernet

Disconnecting your Chromebook from Ethernet is just as easy as connecting it. To avoid the "hot swappable" issue I used this sequence:

- Close the cover of the Chromebook so that power to the USB port is turned off.

- Unplug the "Plugable" adaptor from the USB port on the Chromebook

- Unplug the Ethernet cable from the "Plugable" adaptor

- Open the cover - a WiFi connection will be established automatically.

Figure 2.28 - My Samsung Chromebook with Ethernet Adaptor

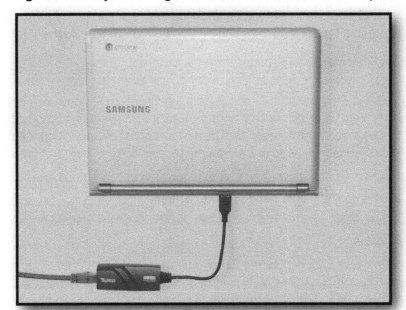

2.8.3 - Using a Mouse with Your Samsung Chromebook

Some people, I'm one of them, prefer to use a mouse rather than the Chromebook's built-in TouchPad. If you would prefer to use a mouse, you could just buy a USB connected mouse and plug that into one of the Chromebook's USB ports. But there is an easy and neater way by using a wireless mouse.

The Logitech M325 Wireless Mouse is one example of such a device. It is available from Amazon for about $20 but it can be found at a lower price from other vendors. I bought mine from Staples for about $15. The Logitech wireless mouse and adaptor are illustrated in Figure 2.29 on the next page. I have included a quarter to show just how small it is.

Set up is easy. Plug the "Nano Receiver" into one of the Chromebook's USB ports. Put batteries in the mouse and turn it on. That's all there is to it. The Chromebook TouchPad continues to work as expected.

Figure 2.29 - Logitech M325 Wireless Mouse and "Nano Receiver"

2.8.4 - Using a Bluetooth Keyboard with Your Samsung Chromebook

Your Samsung Chromebook can connect to different types of Bluetooth devices, but other manufacturer's Chrome Devices may or may not be able to use Bluetooth. To see if your device supports Bluetooth, click on the Status Area in the lower-right corner of the screen - on the photo associated with your Google Account. This will open a menu. If you see the Bluetooth symbol with the words "Bluetooth Disabled" or "Bluetooth Enabled", then your device supports Bluetooth. If you don't see either of these menu items, then your device cannot connect to Bluetooth devices.

As it comes from the factory, Bluetooth is disabled on Samsung Chromebooks. So, to connect a Bluetooth keyboard (or other Bluetooth device) follow these steps:

- Turn on the Bluetooth keyboard (or other device)

- Click on the Status Area photo. This will open a menu with "Bluetooth Disabled" as one item.

- Click on the right-facing arrow and then on "Enable Bluetooth". This will initiate a search for Bluetooth devices.

- When your device name appears in the list of available Bluetooth devices, select it and click on "Connect"

- If you are connecting a Bluetooth keyboard, you will be asked to type a 9-digit PIN on the keyboard. Type this number and hit "Enter". This will pair that keyboard with that Chromebook.

If you have already connected a Bluetooth device, the Bluetooth Control Panel will look like that illustrated in Figure 2.30 on the next page. In this case, I have already connected my Apple Wireless keyboard, named "Administrator's Keyboard", to my Samsung Chromebook. If I wanted to add another Bluetooth device, I would turn that device "on" and then click on the "Add Device ..." button shown in the figure.

Figure 2.30 - The Bluetooth Control Panel

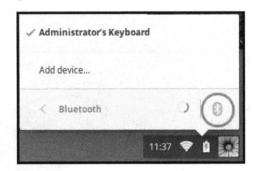

Disabling Bluetooth

If you are not going to be using Bluetooth, you can save battery power by disabling it. To disable Bluetooth and disconnect all devices, click on the Bluetooth symbol circled in Figure 2.30. This will disable Bluetooth.

Re-Enabling Bluetooth

If you want to re-enable Bluetooth and re-connect your Bluetooth devices, just follow the steps described above, with the exception that the Chromebook will remember which devices you have connected in the past and will re-connect them automatically (if they are turned "on"). Type any character on your keyboard to confirm re-connection.

2.8.5 - Using an External Monitor with Your Samsung Chromebook

Samsung Chromebooks have an HDMI output port that you can use to connect your Chromebook to an external computer monitor or TV.

Connecting an External Monitor to Your Chromebook HDMI Port

HDMI ports are not "hot swappable" and so both your Chromebook and the external monitor or TV should be turned off before an HDMI cable is plugged in or unplugged. You may be lucky and get away with "hot swapping" an HDMI connection, but then again, you may not be. So, here's what I do:

- Turn TV or monitor OFF
- Turn Chromebook OFF - hold down the power key for a few seconds
- Connect the HDMI cable to both TV and Chromebook.
- Turn the external monitor or TV ON
- Turn the Chromebook ON.

Following this procedure will not only protect your Chromebook and external monitor from damage, it may also result in fewer problems since the Chromebook may be able to better recognize the TV or Monitor settings if the TV or Monitor is ON when the Chromebook is booted up.

I should mention here that there is a difference between using a TV as an external display and using an actual computer monitor. TVs "overscan" the image presented to them. This means that the top, bottom and right and left sides of the screen image will be cut-off on the TV monitor. They are not cut off on a computer monitor. So, Chrome provides the ability to adjust the size of the image on an external TV so that it all fits on the TV screen. This is a somewhat tricky process and I will try to explain it as best I can a little later.

The Chromebook provides two possible ways to use an external monitor:

- To "Mirror" the Chromebook's display, or
- To "Extend" the Chromebook's display

Using an External Monitor or TV to "Mirror" Your Chromebook Display

You can use an external monitor/TV to "Mirror" your Chromebook display, that is, to display the same stuff on both displays. The Chromebook's display is the "Primary" display and the external monitor or TV simply "mirrors" what is displayed on the Chromebook screen. This mode is only possible if there is a screen resolution on the external display that is "compatible" with the resolution of the Chromebook display. The Samsung Chromebook display has a resolution of 1366 by 768 pixels. Google does not explain exactly what "compatible" means, but I suspect that it means either equal to or an integer multiple of the native Chromebook resolution. If the Chromebook and external monitor/TV cannot negotiate a common resolution, then Mirroring will fail and the external monitor can only be used to "extend" the Chromebook display. This is what usually happens.

At the time this is being written (Chrome Stable Version 28), the use of an external monitor, particularly to "mirror" the main Chromebook display is a work in progress. Sometimes mirroring works but most often it does not. This will differ depending upon which TV you use as the second display. Google is working on this and progress may have been made by the time you read this.

Using an External Monitor or TV to "Extend" Your Chromebook Display

You can use an external monitor/TV to "Extend" your Chromebook's display. With this option, both the Chromebook display and the external display are active and you can move the cursor between them. By default, the Chromebook display is on the virtual left side of your workspace and the external monitor is on the virtual right side. This is true regardless of the real-space arrangement of the displays. There is no virtual space between the two displays - the cursor moves seamlessly between the two displays if you are moving it in the correct direction. Some people experience a lot of frustration because they can't find the cursor when the problem is that they are moving it in the wrong direction. You can change the virtual arrangement of the two displays and I will explain how below.

Setting Up an External Monitor or TV

In the following discussion, I am using a Samsung 21-inch TV as the external monitor.

Connect the HDMI input on the external monitor and the HDMI output on the Chromebook and power up both Chromebook and display as I have described above. At this point your Chromebook display will be the "Primary" display.

In the lower right cornet of the primary display, click on the photo associated with your account to open the Settings menu as illustrated in Figure 2.31. Click on the name of your external monitor. This will open a window where you can "Manage Displays". You can also get to this point by entering the following: Chrome://Settings/Display in the Chrome browser omnibar. The "Manage Displays" window is illustrated in Figure 2.32.

Figure 2.31 - Click on the Name of Your External Monitor

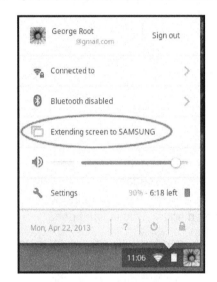

Figure 2.32 - The "Manage Displays" Window

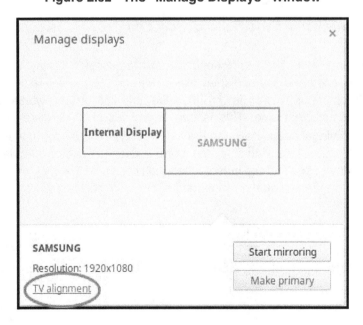

The two rectangles shown in Figure 2.32, labelled "Internal Display" and "Samsung", represent the two displays - showing their relative sizes and virtual arrangement. In this case, "Samsung" refers to the Samsung TV I am using as an external monitor and not to the Samsung Chromebook display. You can make either of the two displays the "Primary" display by clicking on its rectangle and clicking the "Make Primary" button. The "primary" display is the one that controls the action.

By default, the Chromebook display is virtually on the left and the external display is virtually on the right as illustrated in the figure. You can change this virtual arrangement, perhaps to better match their actual physical arrangement, by dragging either rectangle to the other side. The display that you drag will become the "Primary" display.

Clicking on the "Start Mirroring" button shown in Figure 2.32 will initiate a negotiation between the Chromebook and the external display to try and find a "compatible" resolution. This is almost certain to fail. You will probably get an error message that will tell you that Mirroring is not possible and the two displays have been put in "Extended" mode where both monitors are operational.

You can move the cursor between the two "Extended" displays. You can also drag browser windows between them. You can also drag a browser Tab between them and a new Chrome Browser window will open in the display where you drop the Tab. So you can have two different browsers working simultaneously. You can maximize the external display window just as if it were your Chromebook display. In fact, you can do just about anything in the external display that you could do in the Chromebook main display. It is apparent that Google intends this "extended display" mode to allow Chromebook users to use a larger external display, perhaps along with an external keyboard and mouse to simulate a desktop computer.

Adjusting a TV Used as an External Monitor

As I mentioned above, TVs "overscan" the actual physical screen. Because of this, some of the "picture" is cut off. In fact both top and bottom as well as the right and left sides of the screen image are cut off when using a TV as a computer monitor. This is illustrated in Figure 2.33:

Figure 2.33 - A TV Cuts Off Part of the Screen Image When Used as an External Monitor

In this figure, only the portion of the image inside the white border will be displayed on a TV screen being used as an external monitor. This makes it impossible to get to the controls along the lower edge of the screen. For this reason, Google has provided a means for adjusting the size of the image being displayed on the TV.

Clicking on the "TV Alignment" button in Figure 2.32 will open a window as illustrated in Figure 2.34. What this window is trying to communicate is that clicking on the up or down arrow buttons on the Chromebook keyboard will change the vertical size of the displayed image. Clicking on the down-arrow key makes the displayed image smaller in the vertical direction. Similarly, clicking on the right-arrow key makes the TV image smaller in the horizontal direction. You want to make the image smaller in both these directions.

Important Note! You only get one chance to adjust the image size on your external TV monitor. Once you click "OK" in Figure 2.34, you will no longer be able to re-adjust the image size. The only way I have found to "try again" is to "Power Wash" your Chromebook to erase the TV image size settings. You can then start over. Power Washing is described below. Be sure to move any important files out of your "Downloads" folder and into your Google Drive folder before clicking on "OK" because you will lose all the files in your Downloads folder if you do a "Power Wash".

Figure 2.34 - The "TV Alignment" Window Allows You to Compensate for TV Overscan

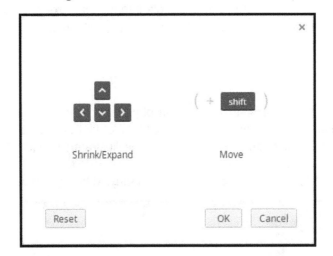

When the TV Alignment window (Figure 2.34) opens, four triangular shaped "arrows" appear in the middle of the four sides of the displayed screen image as illustrated in Figure 2.35 on the next page.

Your objective is to move these triangular arrows inward, toward the center of the screen. You can do that by hitting or holding down the downward pointing arrow key on the keyboard to adjust the vertical size and the right pointing arrow key on the keyboard to make the image smaller in the horizontal direction. Note that the actual image size on the screen does not change. Only the triangular arrows move. You have to guess how far to move them. About as far as shown in Figure 2.35 works on my Samsung TV, but your mileage may vary for different types of TVs. Please read the "Important Note" above before clicking on the "OK" button. If your arrow adjustments don't work as you expected, you may have to "Power Wash" your Chromebook in order to try again.

Figure 2.35 - Triangular "Arrows" Appear on the Sides of the TV Monitor Screen

Once you have adjusted the arrows to your liking, click on the "OK" button in Figure 2.34 and keep your fingers crossed. At this point the image size on the screen will actually change. If things look OK, i.e. if you can use the cursor to click on any of the controls arranged around the outer edge of the screen, then you are done. If not, then you can try to go back to the screen shown in Figure 2.32 and click again on the "TV Alignment" button and start over on your adjustments. This may work in a future Chrome OS update, but it doesn't work with Chrome OS 28. All that happens is that the screen flashes briefly to the state shown in Figure 2.35, but then immediately reverts to the screen size you had previously set.

The only way I have found to "start over" with the TV Alignment process is to "Power Wash" your Chromebook. This will restore your device to its factory settings and, in the process, it will erase your TV Alignment settings. Don't worry, a Power Wash only erases stuff actually stored on your Chromebook. Everything in your Google Drive, all of your installed apps and extensions, and everything else that is synced to Google servers is still there. You just have to sign-in to your Google Account and everything will be restored.

"Power Wash" Your Samsung Chromebook

Power Washing your Chromebook restores it to its factory condition. It has no effect on your Google Account nor on any of your stuff stored in your Google Drive or data that is synced with Google Servers. However, before you Power Wash your Chromebook, you might want to move any files you have stored in your "Downloads" folder since these files actually do reside on your local device and they will be lost during a Power Wash.

The procedure to Power Wash your Chromebook is:

- Click on the Chrome Menu (looks like three horizontal bars in the upper-right corner of the window) and select "Settings". Alternatively, you can click on the photo associated with your account in the lower-right corner of the window and select "Settings". Alternatively, you can type alt + e or alt + f to display the Chrome menu or shift + alt + s to display the Status menu. In any case, select the "Settings" menu item.

- Scroll down to the bottom of the Settings window and click on "Show Advanced Settings"

- At the bottom of the Advanced Settings menu, click on the "Power Wash" button.

- You will be asked to restart your Chromebook. Do it.

- After your Chromebook restarts, you will be asked to confirm that you really want to Power Wash it. Confirm and the Power Washing will begin.

- After the Power Washing is complete, your device will be factory fresh and you will be guided through the process of reconnecting to your WiFi network

- After your network connection is running, you will be asked to agree with the Google Terms and Conditions. Click on "Accept and Continue"

- And, finally, you will sign-in to your Google Account. Remember that the first person to sign-in is the "owner" of that Chrome device. If you enabled Two-Step Authentication when you created your Google Account, you will receive your 6-digit authentication code on your cell phone. Enter that code and click "Verify"

- You will now be given the opportunity to select a photo to associate with your Google Account. Do that and click continue and you will be good to go.

You can now go back to the section titled "**Adjusting a TV Used as an External Monitor**" and try again to adjust your TV image size.

3 - Setting Up a New Google Account

3.3.4 - Google Authenticator

This is an extension of the original Section 3.3.4 which discusses Generating and Printing "Backup Codes". If you have forgotten, "Backup Codes" are part of Google's implementation of "Two-Step Verification". Briefly, with 2-Step Verification enabled, you will need a "secret" one-time PIN to sign-in to your Google Account in addition to the usual User Name and Password. Normally, this secret PIN is delivered to you via text message on your cell phone. But, what if you don't have cell data service where you are? To handle this situation, Google has provided two different ways to obtain a secret PIN without cell phone service. The first method is to generate and print out "Backup Codes" and then to carry those with you if you think you will be out of cell phone coverage the next time you want to sign-in to your account. This whole process is explained in detail in Section 3.3.4.

There is a second way to obtain a secret backup PIN without having to carry one around with you. This method does require that you have a smart phone, but it does not require that you actually have cell phone coverage at the time. This second method relies on a smart phone app called "Google Authenticator". There are Google Authenticator apps available for iPhones, Android phones and Blackberries.

So, the first step in using Google Authenticator is to install the app on your smart phone. You must also have Two-Step Verification enabled for your Google Account, else this whole discussion is pointless.

Initializing Google Authenticator

After you have installed the Google Authenticator app on your smart phone, you have to go to the Google Security page for your Google Account to initialize it. One way to get to this security page is to open any Google service, such as Gmail and sign-in. In the upper-right corner of this window, you will find your Gmail account name as illustrated in Figure 3.10. Click on this name and a menu will drop down with a few options as shown in Figure 3.10. Click on the "Account" item.

Figure 3.10 - The Account Menu is Revealed by Clicking on Your Gmail Address

Clicking on the "Account" item Illustrated in Figure 3.10 will take you to to a menu of Account topics. Click on "Security" and this will take you to a page with a lot of Security settings, a portion of which is shown in Figure 3.11. If your "Status" is not "ON", go back to Chapter 3 and read all about Google Two-Step Verification - you might want to enable it here.

Figure 3.11 - Continue Initializing Google Authenticator by Clicking on "Edit"

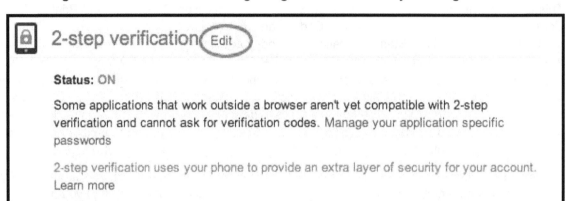

Click on "Edit" as illustrated in Figure 3.11 and that will take you another page with several options, one of which is named "Mobile Application" as shown in Figure 3.12. Select the type of smart phone you want to set-up with Google Authenticator. In my case, I selected "iPhone".

Figure 3.12 - Continue Initializing Google Authenticator by Selecting Your Cell Phone Type

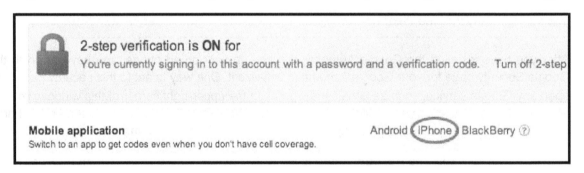

This will (finally) take you to the page where you can initialize your cell phone to provide Google Authenticator Backup Codes. This page is illustrated in Figure 3.13 on the next page. The first part of this page just tells you that you must have the Google Authenticator app installed on your cell phone before going any further.

The real action starts with the instructions:

1) "In Google Authenticator, tap "+", and then "Scan Barcode"

2) "Use your phone's camera to scan this barcode."

Since I have already done these steps, the "+" and "Scan Barcode" buttons don't appear in Figure 3.13, but they will when you go through these steps.

Figure 3.13 - Scan this Bar Code with Your Cell Phone

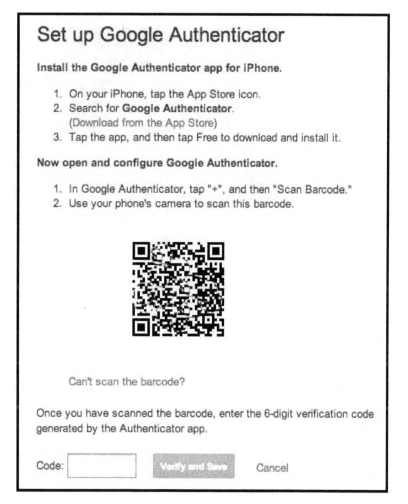

So, launch the Google Authenticator app on your cell phone. Then tap on the "+" to add (generate) another authenticator code and then "Scan Barcode". Now just point your phone's camera at the barcode displayed on your computer screen, just like the one shown in Figure 3.13. You may have to move your camera in and out until it focuses properly on the barcode. When the camera is happy with what it sees, it will take the picture automatically - you don't have to do anything.

When the camera takes the picture of the barcode, a number will appear on the screen of your cell phone. Type this number into the space labeled "Code:" in Figure 3.13 and then click on "Verify and Save". This will complete the setup process. You will get a confirmation that the setup has finished successfully.

Google Authenticator will now be running on your cell phone. Whenever you launch the app, it will generate a new Backup Code and display it as illustrated in Figure 3.14 on the next page.

Figure 3.14 - When You Launch the Google Authenticator App on Your Cell Phone, It will Generate a New Backup Code

These Backup Codes are valid for 1 minute. After that time, a new Backup Code will be generated. The little clock icon shown circled in the upper-left corner of the iPhone screen will count down the 1 minute interval during which the displayed Backup Code remains valid. During the last few seconds remaining, the clock will turn red to let you know that you don't have enough time remaining to enter this Backup Code into whatever app is asking for it, and you should wait until the next code appears.

So, the process for using Google Authenticator goes something like this:

- On your personal computer or Chromebook, you attempt to sign-in to some app that requires Two-Step Verification. That app asks you to enter a 6-digit code that normally would be sent to your cell phone as a text message. But, since you don't have cell phone service at this location, that won't work.

- So, you launch the Google Authenticator app on your cell phone instead. A new 6-digit code will be displayed just as in Figure 3.14. Enter this 6-digit number where the original app on your personal computer is asking for it.

Once again, if you take too long to enter the code number given by Authenticator, you will have to wait until a new number is displayed on the Authenticator screen. You will then have 1 minute to enter this number on your personal computer.

The Verification Codes generated by Google Authenticator are time based, so this process only works if your cell phone is set to the correct time.

Figure 3.14 shows another interesting factoid: Google Authenticator also works with different apps that use Two-Step Verification - not just Google apps. One such 3rd party app is LastPass, my favorite password manager. Clearly, a password manager needs to have a means of secure sign-in. So, LastPass has adopted the Google Authenticator approach to Two-Step Verification. DropBox is another service that uses Google Authenticator.

You set up these 3rd party apps just as you do for the Google apps that I described but with the exception that you must go to the 3rd party app's website to get the proper barcode to scan. For example, the LastPass website is illustrated in Figure 3.15.

Figure 3.15 - Other Apps, Like LastPass and DropBox, Can Use Google Authenticator Too

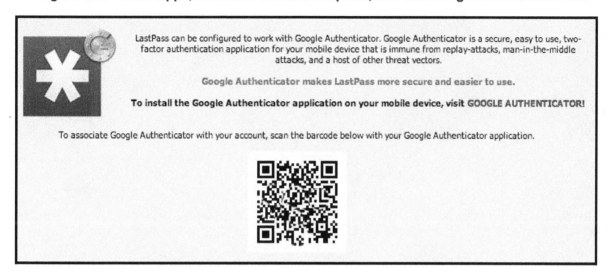

So, looking back at Figure 3.14, you can see that this instance of Google Authenticator has generated two verification codes: one for Google (300163), and one for LastPass (500630). Pretty slick!

Once you start using Google Authenticator, you will no longer receive the 6-digit access codes via text or voice message from Google. When one of these access codes is required, just launch Google Authenticator and use the 6-digit code that it creates for you.

4 - Using Google Drive

4.9 - Hosting a Website Using Google Drive

Hosting a website on Google Drive was discussed briefly in Section 4.9 of the first volume of this book. In this section I will expand upon that topic.

When you create a website, you end up with a file structure similar to that illustrated in Figure 4.6. There is a top level folder, in this case it's named "_BPE Site". This top level folder contains two items: a webpage named "index.html" and another folder which actually contains all of the stuff that makes up your site. This folder is named "Apps" in Figure 4.6 and it is selected to reveal its contents. A site that you want to host on your Google Drive can consist of HTML pages, cascading style sheets (CSS), and Javascript.

The **first step** in hosting your site on Google Drive is to move the top level folder and all of its contents to your Google Drive. Since you probably created your site on your personal computer, you will want to move the site folder into your Google Drive using your personal computer. This is explained in section 4.7, but the brief version is to open the Google Drive folder that appears in your personal computer file system and then drag the site folder ("_BPE Site" in this example) from your personal computer file system into your Google Drive folder. You must have the Google Drive app installed on your personal computer in order for the Google Drive folder to appear in your personal computer file system.

If you have done this using a Mac, the results should look like Figure 4.6:

Figure 4.6 - Typical File Structure for a Website Hosted on Google Drive

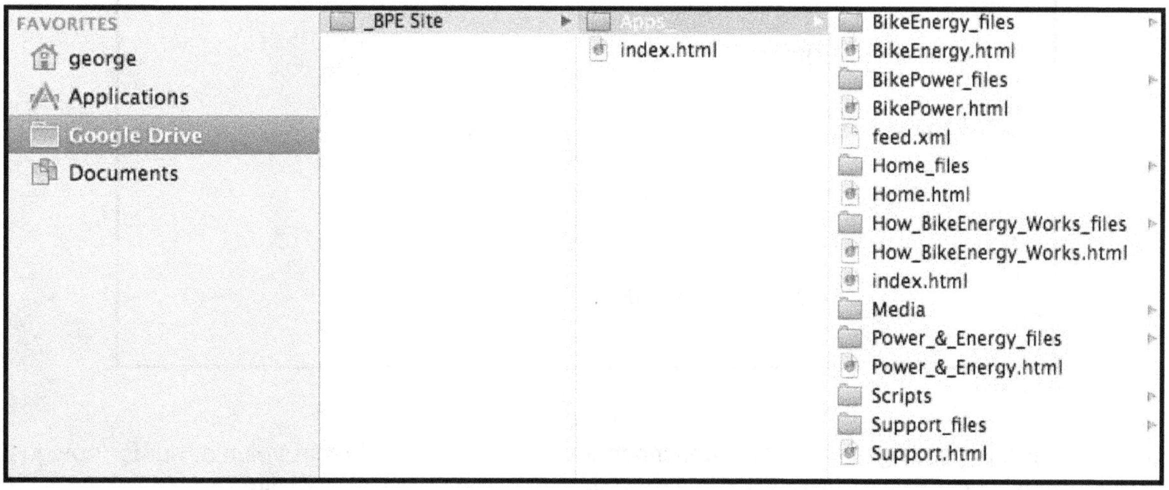

At this point you might have to run the Google Drive app on your personal computer in order to force it to sync with the Google servers. Uploading your site to the Google servers could take a few minutes depending upon how large your site is.

The **second step** in hosting your website is to "Share" the folder containing your site ("_BPE Site" in this example) as "Public on the web". To do this, open the Chrome Browser and navigate to your Drive. If the site has finished uploading to the Google servers, you should see something similar to Figure 4.7

Figure 4.7 - You Must "Share" Your Website Folder

Fist, select the top level folder containing your site ("_BPE Site" in this example) by clicking in the checkbox to the left of the folder name. Then click on the "Share" button - the one that looks like a head and shoulders with a "+" sign as illustrated in Figure 4.7. This will bring up a dialog where you can select various sharing parameters as illustrated in Figure 4.8.

Figure 4.8 - "Share" Your Website Folder as "Public on the Web"

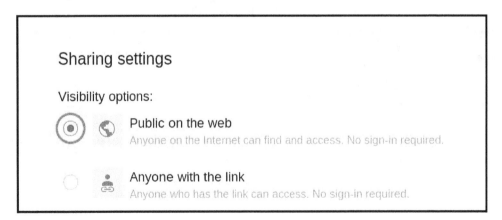

Selecting Sharing settings will be fully described in Section 7.3 later in this Volume, but for now just click on "Public on the Web". This will allow anyone to find and view your website.

The **third step** in hosting your website is to discover the URL that Google has assigned to your site. In order to start this process, go back to your Google Drive and navigate to the "index.html" file that is inside the top level site folder ("_BPE Site") inside the Google Drive folder:

Google Drive -> Top Level Site Folder -> "index.html" file

Click on the "index.html" file to open it. If you expected to see your site, you will be disappointed. What you will see is the html code that represents your site as illustrated in Figure 4.9:

Figure 4.9 - When You Open the index.html File, You Will See HTML Code

```
<?xml version="1.0" encoding="UTF-8"?><!DOCTYPE html PUBLIC "
"http://www.w3.org/TR/xhtml1/DTD/xhtml1-transitional.dtd"><ht
<title></title><meta http-equiv="refresh" content="0;url= App
```

Now, if you look in the lower-right corner of the window containing the html code, you will see a blue button that says "Open" as shown in Figure 4.10. Click on the downward pointing disclosure triangle just to the right of the "Open" button. That should pop-up another button that says "Google Drive Viewer" as shown in Figure 4.10. Click on "Google Drive Viewer". This will open yet another window showing the same html code, but now there is an icon labeled "Preview" as illustrated in Figure 4.11.

Figure 4.10 - Open the "Google Drive Viewer" Button in the Lower-Right Corner of the Page

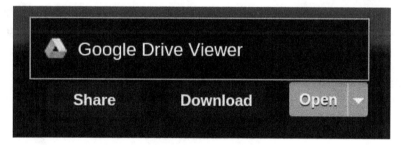

Figure 4.11 - This Time, When You Open the index.html File, There Will Be a "Preview" Icon

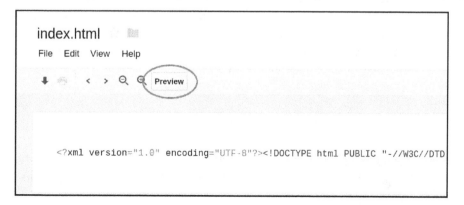

Clicking on "Preview" will, finally, open your website as illustrated in Figure 4.12:

Figure 4.12 - When You Click on "Preview", You Will See Your Actual Website

We're almost there. When you see the home page of your website, you will find the link (URL) that Google has assigned to your site in the Omnibox near the top of the Chrome Browser window. It will start with "https://GoogleDrive.com/host/ ...". Copy that URL - you might also want to Bookmark it so that you can return to your site without all these intermediate steps.

You can now send this link to your website to anyone using an email message and they will be able to see your site by simply clicking on the link. Remember that anyone on the web can also find and view your site.

If you have a relatively simple site and don't expect a lot of visitors, this is a great way to host your site - and it's all free!

4.10 - Sharing Files Using Google Drive

This topic was discussed briefly in Section 7.3 of the first volume of this book. That discussion centered on sharing Google Docs files with others so that they could collaborate with you on creating or editing those documents. But you can share many other types of files using Google Drive, and this new material will tell you how to do that. Because this new material is more closely related to Google Drive itself, I have decided to append it to the original Chapter 4 whose topic was setting up and using Google Drive. Some of this new material will be redundant for which I apologize.

4.10.1 - File Types that Google Drive Can "Share"

There are two categories of files that you can put into your Google Drive. The first category includes file types that the Google Drive Viewer knows how to display. The second category includes file types that the Google Drive Viewer cannot display.

File types that Google Drive **can** display include:

* Native "Google Docs" files: Docs, Sheets, Slides, and Drawings.
* MS Office files: Word documents (.doc, .docx), Excel spreadsheets (.xls, .xlsx), and PowerPoint slide presentations (.ppt, .pptx).
* Image files in: .bmp, .gif, .jpg, .jpeg, .png, and .tiff formats.
* Video files in: .avi, .mov, .m4v, .webm, .wmv, .flv, .3gpp, .mpegps
* Audio files in: .mp3, .mp4, .m4a, .wav, .ogv and some even less popular file types
* Adobe file types: Photoshop (.psd), Illustrator (.ai), Portable Document Format (.pdf)
* Apple file types: Pages (.pages)
* Autodesk AutoCAD (.dxf)
* Plain text files: .txt, .html, .css, .php, .c, .cpp, .h, .php, .js
* PostScript (.eps, .ps)
* Scalable Vector Graphics (.svg)
* Archived files: (.zip, .rar)

So, that's interesting, but what does it have to do with sharing files. "Sharing" in this context means displaying the file so that others can view, comment on, or edit the file contents. If the file type cannot be displayed by Google Drive Viewer, then it cannot be "Shared".

The list of supported file types is always expanding so either check on Google support pages, or just try to share a file. If your attempt to share the file fails, read on for some possible work-arounds.

4.10.2 - Getting Shareable Files into Google Drive

Before you can Share a file with another user, that file must be stored in your Google Drive. Files that you create on your Chrome Device are automatically stored in your Google Drive.

In order to Share a file that you have created on your personal computer, follow these steps:

* Check to be sure that the file you wish to Share is one of the file types listed in Section 7.3.1 above. If it is not, it may be possible to convert it into a "Shareable" file type. For example, if you have created a Numbers document on your Mac, that file type cannot be shared at this time. But, you can export that file from Numbers into an Excel document format file (.xls). This document type can be Shared. The same can be done by exporting Keynote documents in PowerPoint format (.ppt).

   Any file that you can print can be converted into a PDF format file and that file type can be Shared.

* Move the Shareable file to the Google Drive on your personal computer. You can do this by simply dragging it into the Google Drive folder on your personal computer (see section 4.4 in Volume 1 of this book). If you are using a Mac and you hold down the "Option" key when you drag the file, a copy of the file will be placed in your Google Drive. The original file will remain in its original location. On a Windows machine this can be accomplished by Copying the file in its original location and then Pasting it into your Google Drive folder.

❖ Open the Chrome Browser on your personal computer and find the file you just placed in your Google Drive (see section 4.2 in Volume 1 of this book). If the file doesn't appear in your Google Drive, as it usually doesn't, return to your personal computer and run the Google Drive app. Now, when you return to your Google Drive folder using the Chrome Browser on your computer, the file will be there.

OK, at this point you have placed a shareable file into your Google Drive. Now you can set up Sharing for that file.

4.10.3 - Choose the "Visibility" and "Access Privileges" of Shared Files

Visibility: When you share a file or folder in your Google Drive, you will choose the "Visibility" of that file or folder to other people on the web. There are three visibility options:

❖ **Private:** This is the default for newly created files. "Private" files are visible only to you and to other specific people to whom you have granted access to the file. Everyone to whom you grant access must have a Google Account and they must use their sign-in credentials to access the file. This option is useful for sharing "sensitive" documents with a small number of people you know and who all have Google Accounts.

❖ **Anyone with the Link:** As Google says: this is like having an unlisted phone number. Anyone can access the file, but they have to have the exact link (URL) to that file in order to do that. This link cannot be found by searching the web - it will not show up in search results. So, getting the link is not easy - unless someone gives it to you.

When you share a file or folder with "Anyone with the link" visibility, the recipients do not have to have Google Accounts and no sign-in is required to view the file. Anyone who has the link can access the file. This setting is good if you want to share a file or folder with a large group of people and you don't know whether or not they all have Google Accounts.

❖ **Public on the Web:** Files or folders with this visibility can be viewed by anyone. The link to the file or folder will show up in search results and so it can be found by anyone with web access. Use this visibility only if you really do want to make your file or folder visible to everyone.

Access Privileges: When you share a file or folder in your Google Drive, you will also choose "Access Privileges" for each person with whom you have granted access. There are four Access Privilege options:

❖ **Owner:** If you create or upload a file or folder to your Google Drive, you are the "owner" of that file or folder. You can do anything that is possible with that file or folder including: editing the file, deleting the file or folder, adding or removing something to or from a folder. You can grant access to someone else. You can remove access from someone else. And, if you no longer want to own the file or folder, you can transfer ownership to another person.

❖ **Can Edit:** If you grant "Can Edit" access to someone, that person: Can edit the file if it is a Google document - Docs, Sheets, Slides, or Drawings. Can download the file or folder to another device. Can make a copy of the file. Can add and remove items to or from a folder. Can see the list of people to whom you have granted access. "Editors" **cannot** delete the file or folder.

❖ **Can View:** If you grant "Can View" access to someone, that person: Can view files and folders. Can download the file or folder to another device. Can make a copy of the file. "Viewers" **cannot** delete the file or folder.

❖ **Can Comment:** This access is only available for Google documents (Docs) and presentations (Slides). "Commentators" can view and add comments to a Google Doc or Slide presentation. They can download the Google Doc or Slide presentation to another device. They can make a copy of the Google Doc or Slide presentation. They **cannot** delete the file or folder.

One important thing to note is that the combination of "Anyone with the Link" and "Can Edit" gives a lot of power to someone you may not know and who does not have to sign-in in order to edit your document. Anyone to whom you have given "Can Edit" privilege can also (optionally) send a functional link to anyone they know. They can also (optionally) remove people that you have shared the file with. These privileges are "optional" because you will have to decide whether or not to grant these extra privileges when you set up sharing.

OK, with this background we are now ready to start sharing.

4.10.4 - Enable Sharing of a File or Folder in Your Google Drive

If you are creating a "Google Docs" file: Docs, Slides, Sheets, or Drawing, that file will be stored in your Google Drive folder and sharing that file can be done directly from the document itself. Under the "File" menu for Google documents is a item named "Share" as illustrated in Figure 4.13.

Figure 4.13 - Sharing Google Docs Can be Done Within the Document Itself

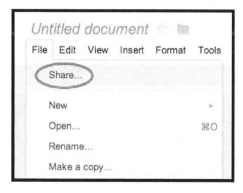

You can also click the big blue "Share" button in the upper-right corner of the document window.

You can also share any shareable file or folder in your Google Drive by following these steps which can be done on your Chrome Device, or on your personal computer running the Chrome Browser:

❖ Open your Google Drive. Refer back to Sections 4.2, 4.3, or 4.4 to refresh your memory of how to do this if necessary.

✤ Right-click (2-finger tap) on the file you want to share and select "Share …" > "Share …" from the pop-up menus that appear as shown in Figure 4.14. You can also select the file you want to share and click on the "Share" icon as explained in Section 7.3

Figure 4.14 - Files and Folders Can Be Shared by Right-Clicking on the File or Folder Name in Google Drive

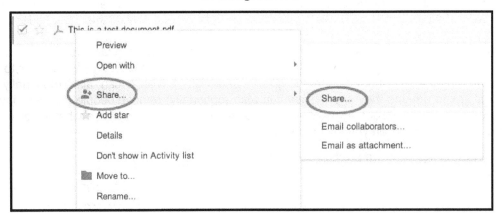

Performing either of these operations: selecting "Share" from a Google Document's File Menu, or right-clicking on the name of a file in Google Drive will bring up a dialog box like the one shown in Figure 4.15 on the next page. This is where you set up all of the sharing options for the file or folder you have selected.

There is a lot of stuff in Figure 4.15 so I have used labels, "A", "B", "C", etc to navigate through all of the options:

(A) This text box is where the magic link to your shared file or folder will appear. People to whom you send this link will be able to access your file or folder.

(B) You can share this link with your recipients via email, Google+, FaceBook, or Twitter.

(C) By default, all files and folders are initially set to be shared as "Private". Refer back to section 4.10.3 for an explanation of what this means.

(D) This is where you will enter the email addresses of the people or groups that you want to share your document(s) with. You can enter individual email addresses or group mailing lists.

(E) You do have to notify your recipients that you have shared a file with them. So, be sure to check the "Notify people via email" checkbox and write a message telling them why you are sharing the document with them. You can also enter any other useful information such as due date here.

(F) By clicking on "Change…" you can change the "Visibility" of the shared file or folder. Refer back to section 4.10.3 for an explanation of what this means.

(G) This is where you get to choose the "Access Privileges" for the file or folder. Once again, refer back to section 4.10.3 for a discussion of what this means.

(H) As I said at the end of section 4.10.3, people with "Can Edit" privilege can add or delete other people to/from the list of recipients. This is a lot of power and it is granted by default. So, you might want to click on the "[Change]" button near the label "H" in Figure 4.15 and revoke this privilege as illustrated in Figure 4.16 on the next page.

Figure 4.15 - Choose Your Sharing Settings in this Window

The default sharing settings shown in Figure 4.15 are Visibility (C) = "Private" and Access Privilege (G) = "Can Edit". These would be good settings if you wanted to allow a few people to collaborate with you on a document you are preparing. However, these would not be good settings if you want to allow a group of people to view, but not change a number of files, photos for example. In this case, you can change Visibility and Access Privilege by clicking on the "Change ..." button (F) in Figure 4.15. This will bring up the window shown in Figure 4.16.

Figure 4.16 - If You Don't Want Editors to be Able to Add and Remove Sharing Recipients, be sure to Revoke that Privilege Here

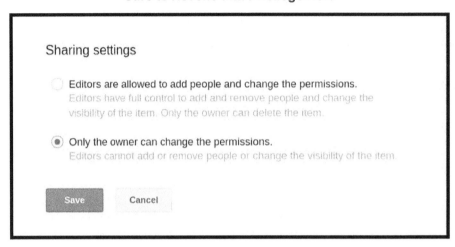

Figure 4.17 - You Can Change Sharing Settings by Clicking on "Change …" (F) in Figure 4.15

In Figure 4.17, you can change "Visibility", who can see the files, by selecting one of the three options: "Public on the web", "Anyone with the link", or "Private". And then, you can select an "Access Privilege" from the pop-up menu "Can View" as illustrated in Figure 4.17, or "Can Edit" (G) in Figure 4.15. These terms are explained in detail in Section 4.10.3.

When you click on the "Share and Save" button at the bottom left of Figure 4.15, the people or group of people whose email addresses you have listed at (D) in Figure 4.15 will be sent an email including the magic link to whatever you are sharing, and the brief message that you entered at (E) in Figure 4.15. Figure 4.18 is an illustration of this message. In this figure I have shared a Google Drawing file named "Guest Pass Flow Chart". All the recipient has to do is click on the "Guest Pass Flow Chart" name embedded in the message.

Figure 4.18 - Your Recipients Will Receive an eMail Message Like This

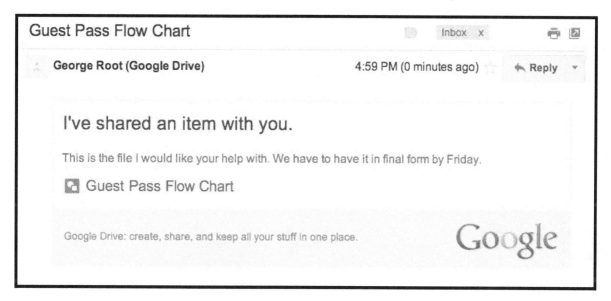

Although clicking on the "Guest Pass Flow Chart" icon used as an example in Figure 4.18 is very simple, it is not so simple to send this icon to others with whom you might want to share this document. It may be easier to simply copy the link to the shared file - see "A" in Figure 4.15 - and send that link to anyone you want to share the file with. For this to work, you must have assigned "Anyone with the Link" as the "Visibility" of the file as is illustrated in Figure 4.17 on the previous page.

5 - Setting Up Google Cloud Print

There are three ways to print documents from Chrome OS devices:

1) Print to a Cloud Print enabled printer

2) Print to a Shared Printer connected to your personal computer

3) Print to a PDF file and then print this PDF file from your personal computer

Each of these approaches is described in some detail in the original Chapter 5. This appendix adds more detail concerning the first printing option: Print to a Cloud Print enabled printer.

Cloud Print enabled printers are relatively new. "Cloud Print enabled" is the Chrome name for this class of printers. Other vendors have different names. Apple calls them "Air Print enabled", HP calls them "ePrint enabled", and so forth. These printers all work the same way and all of them will work with Chrome Devices as well as with iPhones, Android phones, and other internet connected devices.

In the "old days" you connected a printer to your personal computer and installed drivers for that printer on your computer. This approach doesn't work with Chrome OS computers because there are no printer drivers for Chrome. Cloud computing to the rescue. Cloud Print enabled printers are not connected to your computer, but rather to the Internet - possibly through your local area network (LAN). A personal computer is not needed for Cloud Print enabled printers. All of the data and instructions for printing are delivered to the printer via the Internet from a website maintained by the printer's manufacturer. Basically, you send the document you want printed to the manufacturer's website and that website then sends printing instructions directly to your printer. You send the document you want to print as an email attachment to the email address assigned to your printer as will be described below.

Many Cloud Print enabled printers can also work as network shared printers. That is, if you have a local area network and connect a network shared printer to that network, computers that are also connected to your LAN can print directly to the printer without going through the Internet. Printers that can be shared on a LAN are generally identified by the letter "n" appended to their model number. So, for example my HP 401n printer is both a network shared printer as well as a Cloud Print enabled printer. Computers connected to the LAN can print directly to the network printer and Chrome devices can print to the same printer via the Internet.

5.1 - Setting Up a Cloud Print Enabled Printer

Setting up a Cloud Print enabled printer is a three step process described in these sections:

5.1.1) Connect your Cloud Print enabled printer to the manufacturer's website and obtain an unique email address for your printer.

5.1.2) Connect your printer to Google Chrome using the Google Cloud Print Connector

5.1.3) Connect your printer to your iPhone, iPad or Android devices.

5.1.1 - Obtain an Unique eMail Address for Your Cloud Print Enabled Printer

The following description is based on the HP 401n printer. I suspect that setting up other printers from other vendors will work in a similar way. There will be specific instructions for setting up your printer included with the printer.

Step 1) Set up your printer according to the manufacturer's instructions. This will include connecting the printer to your LAN via an Ethernet cable or a WiFi network connection.

Important Note: If you connect your printer to your personal computer using a USB or other cable, it cannot be used as a Cloud Print Enabled printer. You must connect your Cloud Print Enabled printer directly to a network that has Internet access, not to a computer.

Near the end of the setup process, the printer will print out a page of information. This information contains two important items:

1) The IP address assigned to the printer by your router. For example, my HP 401's LAN address is 10.0.1.193. You will need this IP address to connect with the printer's built in website.

2) A "Claim Code" that identifies your printer to the manufacturer in order to obtain an email address for that specific printer.

You might want to keep this information for future reference.

Step 2) Using any LAN connected computer, for example your Chromebook, enter the printer's IP address in the Omnibar of the Chrome Browser. So, for example, I entered 10.0.1.193 in the Omnibar of my Chrome browser. This will connect you to a web page that is built into your printer. This web page will allow you to make various settings and to check on things like toner or ink supply levels.

With the HP 401n printer, this built in web page also allows me to connect to the "HP Web Services" website. The first thing I had to do on this site was to accept the "Terms of Use" to enable HP Web Services. This took me to the "HP ePrint Center". You will, of course, go to the website for your particular brand of printer - not necessarily to the HP site.

Step 3) Create an "HP Connected Account". This involves entering a valid email address and creating a password. You must also agree to the "HP Connected Terms of Use".

Step 4) Add your device to your HP Connected Account. This will require the "Claim Code" that the printer printed at the end of Step 1. I gave HP my Claim Code and HP gave me an unique email address for my printer. My printer's email address looks like **********@hpeprint.com . You will have the opportunity to change this address if you choose to. You definitely want to save this address. You will need it every time you print something. I entered this address into my Contacts list using the name "HP Printer". So, whenever I want to print something, I can just email it to "HP Printer".

Step 5) Limit ePrint access to your printer. Right now, anyone that has your printer's email address can send stuff and your printer will print it. This could turn into the print version of spam. To prevent this from happening, you can limit access to your printer to just a few "From" email addresses.

Remember that to print a document you attach it to an email message and send that message to your printer's email address. The email address from which you send the message is the "From" address. So, if you send your email messages from your Gmail account, it is that Gmail account address that you will use to limit access to your printer. HP Connect allows you to enter a list of email addresses that are allowed to print to your printer. You will probably enter all the email addresses that you and any family members or fellow workers use so that they can all print to your printer. HP will send a confirmation message to all of the email addresses you list.

That's it. Your Cloud Print enabled printer is now all set up. You can test it by composing a brief email message and sending it to your printer's email address. After a brief wait, the message should be printed. If this doesn't work, you will have to refer to your printer vendor's support site for help.

Important Note: If you enter any text in the body of an email message, that is what will get printed. Any attachment will be ignored. So, if you want to print a document, attach it to a blank email message.

5.1.2 - Connect Your Printer to Google Chrome Using the Google Cloud Print Connector

At this point you can print to your Cloud Print Enabled printer by attaching the document to be printed to an email message and then sending that message to your printer's email address. That works, but it becomes cumbersome if you want to print several documents. Fortunately, there is an easier way. If you connect your printer to your Google Cloud Print Account, then that printer will appear in the list of possible printers when you select "Print" when using any application.

Google Cloud Print is still a work in progress, so what you see on your screen may be slightly different from what is shown in the following figures.

To connect your Cloud Print Enabled printer, you will have to visit the Chrome Cloud Print Settings page:

- Launch the Chrome Browser
- Click the "3-horizontal bar" icon near the upper right of the window and select "Settings"
- Near the bottom of the Settings window click "Show Advanced Settings"
- Scroll down to "Google Cloud Print" and click on "Manage Print Settings ..." as shown in Figure 5.1. If you have never connected a printer before, this button will be labeled "Open Cloud Print"

**Figure 5.1 - You Can Add Your Printer to Google Cloud Print
by Clicking on "Manage Print Settings"**

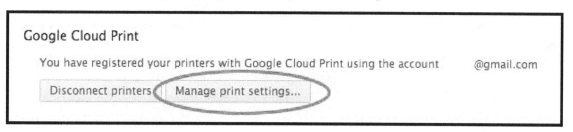

This will open a page, part of which is illustrated in Figure 5.2. Just click on "Add a Cloud Ready Printer"

Figure 5.2 - Click on Add a Cloud Ready Printer

That will take you to another page, part of which is illustrated in Figure 5.3.

Figure 5.3 - Select the Manufacturer of Your Cloud Ready Printer

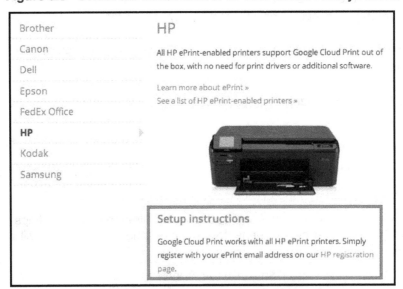

On the page illustrated in Figure 5.3, first select the manufacturer of your Cloud Ready Printer. This will display a screen specific to your type of printer. The page illustrated in Figure 5.3 is specific to HP printers, so what you see may be quite different. The "Setup Instructions" shown in Figure 5.3 end with the admonition to click on the "HP Registration Page" link. Do that and it will take you to a site specific to your printer. The one illustrated in Figure 5.4 is specific to HP printers.

Figure 5.4 - You Can Connect Your Printer to Google Cloud Print

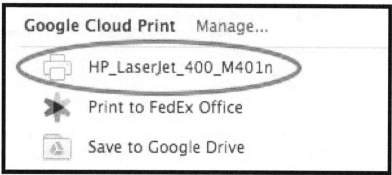

Simply fill in the email address assigned to your printer and click on "Connect My Printer". That's all there is to it. If everything has worked out as expected, you will now see your Cloud Ready printer listed as one of the destinations for any document you print as is illustrated in Figure 5.5

Figure 5.5 - Your Printer Now Appears in the List of Available Print Destinations

At this point, you no longer have to send documents as email attachments in order to have them printed. Just call up the print dialog by typing ctrl+p (hold down the ctrl key while typing "p") in any app that supports printing and select your Cloud Enabled printer from the list of possible destinations as is illustrated in Figure 5.5.

5.1.3 - Connect Your Printer to Your iPhone, iPad, Windows 8, or Android Device

----

At this point you can print to your Cloud Print Enabled printer from your Chromebook. But Cloud Print Enabled printers can also be used with other wireless devices such as iPhones, iPads, and Android devices. These devices are like Chromebooks in that you cannot connect a printer directly to the device itself. These devices all print in exactly the same way that the Chromebook does. They all send the document to be printed to the Cloud Enabled printer's email address. And, just as with Chromebooks, there is an easier way to accomplish this so that you don't have to actually send an email attachment yourself. There's a app for that.

In order to connect your iPhone, iPad, Windows 8, or Android device to your Cloud Enabled printer, you must install an app that is specific to your type of printer as well as being specific to your wireless device. So, for iPhones and iPads to be able to print to an HP ePrint Enabled printer, you must install one of the "HP ePrint" apps available free from the iTunes Store > App Store. If your printer is a LaserJet, you want to install the "HP ePrint" app. If you have a DesignJet printer, you want the "HP DesignJet ePrint" app. There will be other apps specific to other types of printers. For example, if you have an Epson iPrint Enabled printer, you will install the "Epson iPrint" app.

If you have an Android device, you will get your Cloud Print app from the Google Play Store. Once again, the apps needed to print to HP or Epson printers are called "HP ePrint" and "Epson iPrint" respectively. Windows 8 devices have the printing apps already installed so you don't have to do anything except to be sure that both your Windows 8 device and your printer are both connected to the same WiFi network.

The first time I ran the HP ePrint app on my iPhone, it asked for my email address. That is, the email address I used when I set up my HP Connected Account as described above, not the address of my printer. The HP servers than sent a PIN to that email address and asked me to enter that PIN on the screen of my iPhone. Once I did that and touched "Activate", I was all setup.

Exactly how you go about printing from your mobile device depends upon the device. HP has a nice website with a series of short videos showing how to print to HP ePrint enabled printers from the various mobile device types: iOS, Android, Windows 8, and BlackBerry. Things should work the same with other types of printers. The link to the HP site is:

http://www.hp.com/united-states/campaigns/mobility/#apple-tab

And a portion of that site is shown in Figures 5.6 and 5.7 on the next page. This series of steps summarizes how to print from an iOS device and from an Android device to an HP ePrint enabled printer. Once again, things should work the same way if you have a different type of printer.

Figure 5.6 - A Portion of the HP Site Summarizing How to Print from iOS Devices

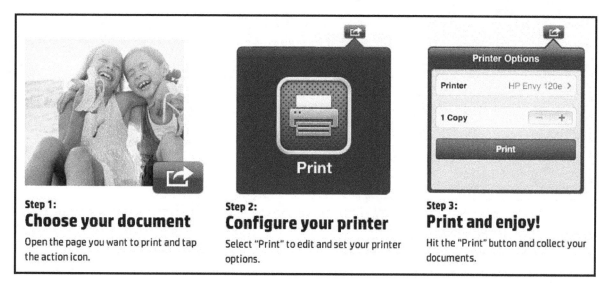

Step 1:
Choose your document
Open the page you want to print and tap the action icon.

Step 2:
Configure your printer
Select "Print" to edit and set your printer options.

Step 3:
Print and enjoy!
Hit the "Print" button and collect your documents.

Figure 5.7 - A Portion of the HP Site Summarizing How to Print from Android Devices

Step 1:
Download the HP ePrint app [4]
Once the app is downloaded, locate it in your device's app gallery.

Step 2:
Open the app and choose your document
Confirm your printer settings and select "Print."

Step 3:
Print and enjoy!
Once you've hit "Print," you'll have the option to change your printer once more.

Important Note: Remember that when you print a document to a Cloud Enabled printer from any vendor and from any device, that document gets transmitted to the printer vendor's servers where it is stored briefly during the printing process. All of the printer vendors say that they will delete your document as soon as the print job has finished, but who knows? Don't print anything that you consider "sensitive" using any Cloud Enabled printer. Better to "print" it to a PDF file and then transfer that to your personal computer using a USB drive. You can then print that file to a printer connected to your personal computer.

12 - Google+

12.1 - What is Google+ ?

Google+ is HUGE! At this time, Google+ is the second largest social networking site in the world.

The name "Google+" encompasses so many different, but related, services that there are entire books written about this one topic. It will not be possible to cover all of the aspects of Google+ in this chapter - to be perfectly honest, there are parts of Google+ that I don't even understand. But, I do think that what is presented in this chapter will give you a good start in setting up and using the many services that are collectively known as Google+.

If you are familiar with Facebook or Twitter or LinkedIn or any of the other "social" services that are so popular on the Internet, then you will recognize that Google+ is similar to them. In fact Google+ combines many of the features of all these services along with Skype into a single, elegant package.

The basic concept of Google+ is that you will create groups of friends and acquaintances with whom you can share your thoughts, ideas, photos, videos, links to interesting web pages, and more. Google calls these groups of people "Circles".

Or you can find "Communities" of people who share the same interests you do.

Or you can "Follow" your favorite tech company (Google of course) or actress (not literally).

Or, you can make video conference calls with members of your Circles using a part of Google+ called "Hangouts".

The main components of Google+ are illustrated in Figure 12.1. We will start our discussion at the left side of this figure with your Google+ "Profile". When you set up your Profile, you join Google+ .

Figure 12.1 - The Components of Google+

12.2 - Setting Up Your Google+ Profile

Your Google+ Profile can contain a lot, or not so much, information about who you are, what your interests are, where you went to school, where you work, and a lot more. Personally, I tend toward the "not so much" end of this spectrum. My friends already know who I am and I'm not all that comfortable telling strangers all of my personal information. The benefit of sharing a lot of information about yourself is that it might help other people to "find" you. For example, You might like to find people with whom you worked in your first job. Google+ allows you to find these people, but you can only do that if they have included their job histories in their public Profiles. And it works both ways. They will not be able to find you unless you include your job history in your Profile. So, Google+ lets you choose how much or how little you want to share with other people.

There are several different ways to access your Profile setup page on Google+. One of these ways is to go to:

https://plus.google.com/

Or you can add the free Google+ app to your Chromebook or Chrome Browser. You will find it in the Chrome Web Store - see Section 2.7 in the original volume for a discussion of the Chrome Web Store.

Figure 12.2 - The Google+ App is Available from the Chrome Web Store

Once you have installed the Google+ app, the Google+ icon will appear in the list of apps installed on your computer. You can then get to your Google+ Home page by simply clicking on this app icon as illustrated in Figure 12.3.

Figure 12.3 - You Can Go To Your Google+ Home Page by Clicking this App Icon

When you click the Google+ app icon, that will open your Google+ Home page, the top-left portion of which is illustrated in Figure 12.4 on the next page. When the page opens, you will probably see only the "Google+" and the "Home" items at the top of Figure 12.4. Just hover your cursor over the "Home" icon and the rest of the menu items will appear. Select "Profile" to edit your Google+ Profile.

Figure 12.4 - A Portion of the "Home Page" of Your Google+ Account

Clicking on the "Profile" menu item in Figure 12.4 will take you to a page, the top portion of which is illustrated in Figure 12.5. There are several parts to the portion of the page shown in Figure 12.5. First, there is a row of tabs along the top edge of the figure. The "Posts" tab is open by default. Right now we want the "About" tab which will take us to a page "about" you - that is your Google+ Profile. But before we leave this page, there are a couple of other things to point out.

Figure 12.5 - This is the Top Portion of Your Google+ Home Page

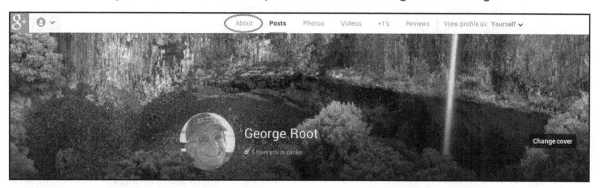

You may have already supplied a photo of yourself when you created your Google Account. If you have, it will appear near the center in your version of Figure 12.5. If you hover the cursor over the photo of yourself, a small camera icon will appear and clicking on this will take you to a page where you can select a different photo to be used as "you".

The pretty picture of a waterfall is called the "cover" of your Profile page. You can change this photo by clicking on the "Change Cover" button at the right in Figure 12.5.

Lastly, the item at the far right end of the tab bar labeled "View Profile as: Yourself" will reveal a drop-down menu allowing you to choose how you want to "see" your profile. "As Yourself" means that you will be able to "see" everything in your profile. "Public" means that you will be able to see only those Profile items that you have shared with the "Public". "Public" information can be found by search engines, like Google, and can be read by anyone.

Clicking on the "About" tab in Figure 12.5 will (finally) open your actual Profile page as illustrated in Figure 12.6. I have modified this figure to conserve space while still showing a portion of the types of information you can enter into your Profile.

Figure 12.6 - A Slightly Modified Version of Your Google+ Profile Page

The full Profile page is very large with a lot of stuff that you can fill in to describe yourself to other Google+ users. I will list just a few of the major topics that you can fill in if you choose to:

1) Lists of people you have in your Circles or who have you in their Circles.
2) Your Work history : Occupation, Skills, and Employment History
3) Places you have been
4) Your personal "Story": Tagline, Introduction, and "Bragging Rights"
5) Education
6) Basic Information: Gender, Who you are "looking for", Who you are in a "Relationship" with.
7) Your Contact Information: Home and Work
8) Some other bits and pieces of who you are

One portion of the Profile page is shown in Figure 12.7 on the next page. This particular panel allows you to enter your Educational information. The other panels operate in the same way. You can fill in or edit any or none of the Profile information that you choose to on this page. The only information that is required is your full name and that will be shared with the "Public" - you cannot change that. Be sure to click on "Save" after you have made any changes.

Once again there is a drop-down menu which is circled in Figure 12.7 that controls the visibility of your Profile information in this panel - the Educational panel in this example. The default is to share your information with the "Public" , that is with anyone who happens to stumble across your Google+ Profile. If you don't want to share this information with everyone, you can limit access to your Profile information on a panel by panel basis. That is, you can choose one visibility for your Educational information and a different visibility for your "Work" information. This is described in the next section.

Figure 12.7 - You Can Limit the Visibility of Your Profile Information

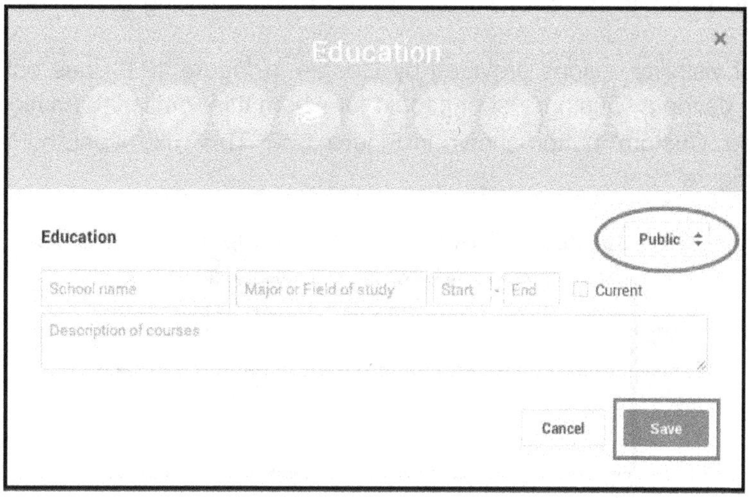

12.3 - Limiting Access to Your Google+ Profile

Because your Profile may contain information that you do not want to share with everybody (Public), Google+ allows you to limit the visibility of each category of information in your Profile. Figure 12.7 illustrates this for the "Education" section of your Profile. The other sections work the same way.

The "Public" item that is circled in Figure 12.7 indicates that all of your Education information (in this example) is "Public" by default. "Public" information is visible to just about anyone. If you don't want this visibility, you can limit the people who can "see" this category of information by clicking on the "Public" drop-down menu shown circled in Figure 12.7. This will reveal a menu of options for limiting the visibility of the information in the selected category as illustrated in Figure 12.8.

Figure 12.8 - Clicking on "Public" Reveals a Menu of Visibility Options

In this menu, you can choose to share the information with your "Extended Circles", with just "Your Circles", with "Only You" (I'm not sure what this accomplishes), or with a "Custom" subset of people. I will discuss "Circles" more completely in the next section, but for now, a "Circle" is just a group of people you have selected on the basis of common interests or because they have some specific relationship to you - for example "Co-Workers" might be one of your Circles. The list shown in Figure

12.8 is the default list provided by Google. You will be able to define and populate your own Circles to include anyone you want to include. I will discuss this in the following section on "Circles".

If the default list of visibility options provided by Google in Figure 12.8 does not include what you want, then you can define a "Custom" list of people for whom this Profile information will be visible. To do this, click on the "Custom" button shown in Figure 12.8. This will reveal the "Add More People" button outlined in Figure 12.9.

Figure 12.9 - Clicking on "Custom" Allows You to Add People Who Can "See" this Information

Clicking on "Add More People" will take you to the list illustrated in Figure 12.10 where you can select which Circles of people you want to be able to see this information.

Figure 12.10 - Clicking on "Add More People" Reveals a List of All Your Circles

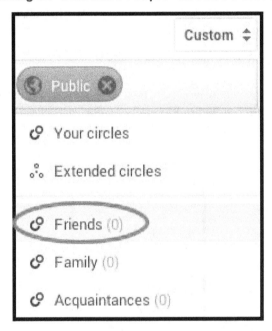

I know this is a little confusing. You have to create your custom "Circles" of people before you can add them to the list of people who can view your Profile information. But, I haven't discussed how to do that yet. I will in the next section. For right now, just pretend that you have created some custom Circles and given them names like "Work Buddies", "My Wife's Friends", " People to Avoid", etc. These names of Circles will appear in the list of Circles illustrated in Figure 12.10. You can even create a Circle that contains only a single person. So, you can limit access to some of your Profile information to just one other person if you want to.

In Figure 12.10 I haven't created any custom Circles yet so all you see are the default Circles suggested by Google. Let's just say, as an example, that I would like to share my Education Profile information with my "Friends" and "Acquaintances" Circles. Note that the numbers in parentheses following the names of the Circles in Figure 12.10 tell how many people are in each Circle. Actually, in Figure 12.10 both of these Circles are empty (0). I haven't put any people in them yet. I'm waiting until the next section where I will explain how this is done. For right now, just imagine that there really are people in these Circles.

So, to accomplish my goal of making my Educational information visible to my "Friends" and "Acquaintances", I need to do four things:

1) Click on the "Friends" Circle name shown outlined in Figure 12.10

2) Click on "+ Add More People" in the panel that appears

3) Click on the "Acquaintances" Circle name

4) Click on the "X" just to the right of the "Public" Circle name at the top of Figure 12.10

If you don't delete the "Public" Circle, your information will still be visible to everybody. The net result of all these clicks is illustrated in Figure 12.11 which shows that this portion of my Profile (the Education information in this example) will be visible only to those people in my "Friends" and "Acquaintances" Circles, just as I wanted.

Figure 12.11 - This Profile Information Will Be Visible Only to Those People in the "Friends" and "Acquaintances" Circles

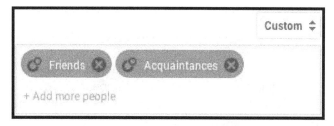

So, you can put a lot of "sensitive" information in your Profile but limit what people can see it. And you can put different limits on the different categories of Profile information. For example, you can limit your work information to just those people you work with and your relationship information to just your best friends (who probably already know anyway). Just be aware that no matter how you limit your information's visibility, there are two entities that can see everything you enter: Google and the NSA.

12.4 - Your Google+ "Home Page"

Your Google+ Home Page is the hub of all your Google+ activities. This is where you can customize your Google+ experience, where you will see the stuff that has been shared with you, and where you can share stuff with other people. Because you will be returning to your Home page frequently, I thought it might be useful to discuss how to get to your Home page. There are several ways to do this. I have already touched on two of these ways in Section 12.2: goto https://plus.google.com/ in any web browser, or if you are using the Chrome Browser or OS, you can install the Google+ app as described in Section 12.2.

A third and sometimes easier way is a direct link to your Google+ Home Page that is available on most Google service pages. For example, Figure 12.12 shows the Google+ link which is near the upper-right corner of a New Tab browser page.

**Figure 12.12 - Clicking on the +Your Name Button
Will Take You to Your Google+ Home Page**

Clicking on the +YourName button should take you to your Home Page, but sometimes Google makes a stop before you get there to remind you to add more people to your Circles. If this happens, just click on the "Continue to Google+" button near the bottom of the page as illustrated in Figure 12.13.

Figure 12.13 - If Google Sidetracks You, Just Click on "Continue to Google+"

Your Google+ Home Page is where "Posts" sent to you will appear. If you are a member of a "Community", the Posts sent to that Community will appear on your Home Page. If you are "Following" someone, posts from that person or entity will appear on your Home Page. I'll explain all those quoted words a little later. Your Home Page is also where you will create and send Posts (text, photos, videos, links to web pages) to people in your Circles.

Once you get to your Home Page, you will find in the upper-left corner a button labeled "Home". If you hover your cursor over this button, a drop-down menu containing links to all of the Google+ stuff you might want to go to becomes visible. This drop-down menu is illustrated in Figure 12.14 on the next page.

We have already used this drop-down menu to get to the Profile page described in Section 12.2. This drop-down menu will be like a roadmap for the following discussions. At this point, we have discussed creating your Google+ Profile - the link to which is just below the "Home" button. Just below the Profile button is a button labeled "People" with a little icon that looks like two linked circles. This is the button that takes you to a page where you can create and populate your "Circles" of friends, acquaintances, and other people. This is discussed in the next section.

Figure 12.14 - Hovering the Cursor Over the "Home" Label on Your Google+ Home Page Reveals the Menu of Google+ Activities

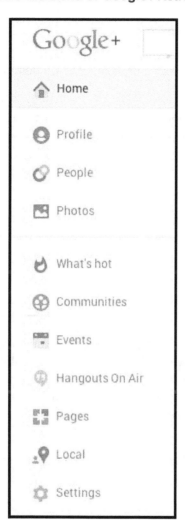

12.5 - Creating and Populating Your Google+ Circles

Circles are just groups of people. You can create Circles and populate them with people you know or people you find using Google+. When you share something on Google+, you can share it with a single person, or you can share it with one of your Circles, that is you can share it with a whole group of people at one time. Your Circles will consist of other Google+ users. If you have a friend that you would like to add to one of your Circles, that friend has to have a Google+ account (Profile) before you can add them to your Circles.

When you create a Circle and add someone to it, you are starting a linked list of people. This list starts with the people you add to your Circles. The list continues to spread outward to include all the people in their Circles. These are called your "Extended Circle". As you can imagine, you can rapidly find yourself sharing stuff with people you never heard of. So, be careful when you add people to your Circles. You may be sharing with their friends as well as your own.

12.5.1   Creating New Google+ Circles

Google provides all Google+ users with a default set of Circles to get you started. This default set is illustrated in Figure 12.15.

Figure 12.15 - Google Provides a Default Set of Circles for You

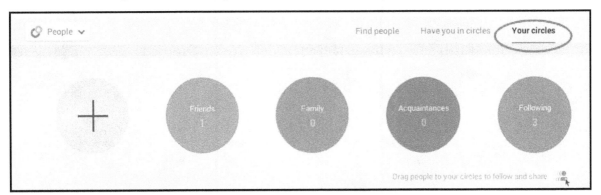

To get to this page, you first hover your cursor over the "Home" button on your Google+ Homepage. This will drop down the menu shown in Figure 12.14. Click on the "People" button in this menu. You can see in Figure 12.15 that we are on the "People" page because of the "People" label in the upper-left corner. There are three "tabs" displayed at the top of Figure 12.15: "Find People", "Have You in Circles", and "Your Circles". I have selected the "Your Circles" tab in this figure. This is where you can create and populate your Circles.

The default set of Circles that Google provides are: "Friends", "Family", "Acquaintances", and "Following". "Friends" and "Family" are pretty self explanatory, but what the heck is "Following"?

Figure 12.16 - Hovering Your Cursor Over a Circle Reveals Information About that Circle

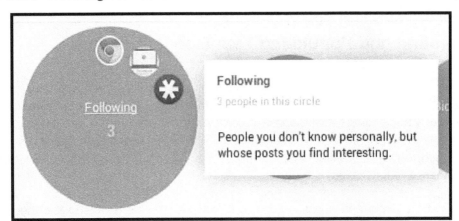

As illustrated in Figure 12.16, if you hover your cursor over one of the Circle icons, the Circle icon will expand and reveal information about that Circle. In this case, we find that my "Following" Circle contains three "people" and that, according to Google, these are "people" I don't know personally, but whose posts I am "Following". As you can see, these aren't actually people, but rather blog-like entities that post things related to three things I am interested in: the Chrome OS, Chromebooks, and the LastPass password manager app. Adding an "entity" rather than a real person to your Following Circle is like subscribing to an rss feed or blog. But, of course, you can also add real people to your "Following" Circle - perhaps your favorite singer or actor, for example.

OK, Google provides a default set of Circles, but now we want to create some new Circles of our own. In case you couldn't guess, that gray Circle with the big plus sign at the left side of Figure 12.15 is one way to create a new Circle. Clicking on this "New Circle" button opens a page where you can give your new Circle a name. This is illustrated in Figure 12.17.

Figure 12.17 - Clicking on the Big Plus Button Creates a New Circle

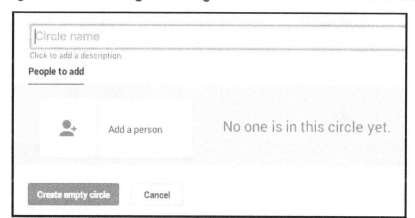

You can type in a name for the new Circle. For example, I created a Circle that I named "Chrome Buddies". I intend to add a few friends who are also interested in the Chrome OS and Chromebooks. I wouldn't want to annoy most of my friends who still think that "Chrome" is something you plate old auto bumpers with. So I'm creating a small Circle of friends with whom I can share "Chrome" stuff without boring all of my other friends. As shown in Figure 12.17, you can also add a description of your new Circle in case you forget why you created it.

At this point, you can click on "Create Empty Circle" to do just that. A new Circle will be created and you will be able to add people later. Or, if you know who you want to add to this Circle, you can do that by clicking on the "Add a Person" button in Figure 12.17. This will open a panel as illustrated in Figure 12.18.

Figure 12.18 - Clicking on "Add a Person" Allows You to Do That

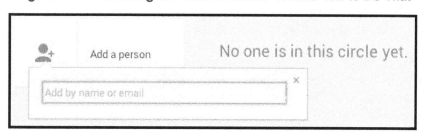

12.5.2 Populating Google+ Circles

One way to populate a new Google+ Circle is to type the name or email address of a person you would like to add into the box illustrated in Figure 12.18. You can repeat "Add a Person" as many times as you like to populate your new Circle. You can only add people who also have a Google+ account Profile. If you would like to add someone who doesn't have a Google+ account, Google suggests that you invite them to join.

There are other ways to find people to add to your Circles. Google is happy to help you find these people. Going back to the "People" page illustrated in Figure 12.15 and selecting the "Find People" tab opens a window where you can use several different Google tools to find people to add to your Google+ Circles.

Figure 12.19 - Clicking on "Find People" Opens a Window Where Google Will Help You Find People to Add to Your Circles

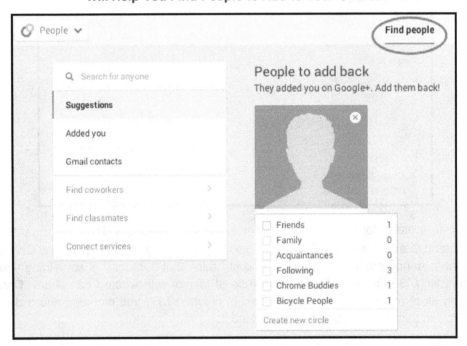

As you can see in Figure 12.19, there is a menu at the left side of the figure and the item "Suggestions" has been selected. In Figure 12.19 I have shown only a single "suggested" person, but in reality there are hundreds of suggestions, many of which are completely unknown to me. In this illustration, the suggested person has been suggested because she had added me to one of her Circles. Google+ is suggesting that I add her back. When you click on a person, a drop-down menu appears providing a list of all your Circles. You can select one or more Circles to add this person to.

Also shown in Figure 12.19, the last item in the drop-down menu of your Circles is an item "Create New Circle". This is a second way to create and populate a new Google+ Circle, starting with a person rather than with a new Circle. So, you can create a new Circle as described in section 12.5.1 and then add people to that Circle, or you can start with a person and create a new Circle "around" that person. In either case, once you have created a Circle, the name of that Circle will appear in the drop-down list of your Circles whenever you select a person to add.

Figure 12.19 illustrates the case where Google+ makes "Suggestions" for people you might like to add to one of your Circles. There are other lists of people that Google+ will provide and these are shown in the menu at the left of Figure 12.19.

The second list of people Google+ thinks you might like to add to your Circles consists of people who have added you to one of their Circles. Google+ suggests that you might like to "add them back". I will discuss the implications of adding or of being added to a Google+ Circle in the next section.

Some ways that Google+ can help you find people are:

- People who have added you to one or more of their Circles
- People in their Circles
- People in your Contacts list
- Co-Workers
- Classmates
- Real estate and insurance salesmen trying to find customers

12.5.3   What Happens When You Add Someone to Your Google+ Circles

The whole point of adding people to your Circles is so that you will be able easily to share stuff with them and to have their stuff shared with you. You can share stuff by "Posting" to one of your Circles. Everyone in that Circle will be able to see your "Post" which can contain text, photos, videos, calendar events, and links to web pages you think they might find interesting. In order for them to see your Posts, you have to be in one of their Circles. That's why Google+ suggests that you "add them back" when someone adds you to one of their Circles. This establishes the two-way link that allows the two of you to exchange Posts.

Figure 12.20 - To Share Posts You Must be in Each Other's Circles

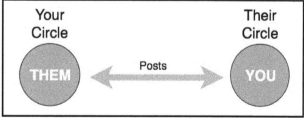

OK, that's the good part of adding someone to your Circles. There are also some perhaps unintended consequences of doing that:

- When you add someone to one of your Circles, they receive a notification that you have done that and a suggestion that they "add you back". Although they get notified that you have added them to one of your Circles, they do not get to see the name of that Circle.

- When someone adds you to one of their Circles, you can "see" who else is in the Circle they added you to. You might want to add one of their friends to your Circle. This also means that if you add someone to one of your Circles, they can see who is in your Circle.

- You cannot prevent another Google+ user from adding you to their Circles, but you can block any communications from them.

12.5.4 Adding "Communities" to Your Google+ Circles

Generally your Circles will be composed of people you know, only 1 or 2 "degrees of separation" from you. But you might also like to share stuff with people that you don't know, but who have some of the same interests that you do. This is where Google+ "Communities" comes in.

Referring back to Figure 12.14, about half way down the menu of Google+ activities, there is an item named "Communities". Clicking on the "Communities" menu item will open a window that shows dozens or hundreds of Communities you might like to add to your Circles. Just a few of these are shown in Figure 12.21

Figure 12.21 - Selecting the "Communities" Item in the Google+ Menu Opens this Page

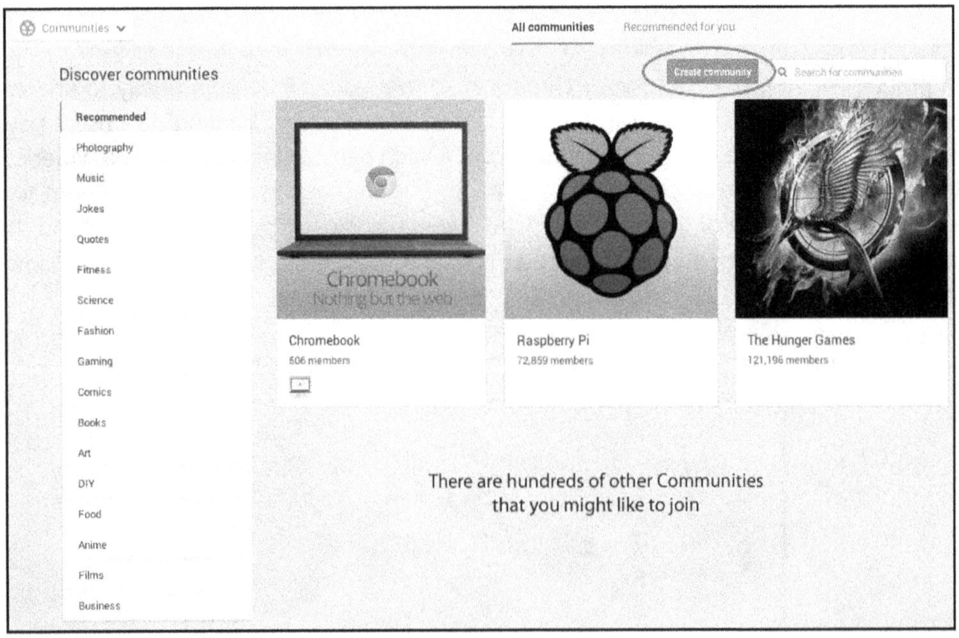

Communities are groups of people that share a common interest. For example, in Figure 12.21 there are Communities of people who are interested in Chromebooks, Raspberry Pi, and the Hunger Games. Google Communities are like the old Google Groups (see Chapter 10 in the original volume) or discussion forums. You can read what other people are saying about the Community topic, or you can contribute by adding your own post or question or by commenting on an existing post.

Along the left edge of the Communities page illustrated in Figure 12.21 is a menu of top level topics such as "Science" or "Fashion" to help you narrow your search for a specific topic that interests you.

Selecting (clicking on) one of the suggested Communities in Figure 12.21 will open a page devoted to that specific Community. For example, in Figure 12.22 I have selected a Community named "Google Chrome". This page gives a brief description of the Community's purpose, the number of people in this Community, a sample of recent posts to the Community, and (optionally) a list of the names of all the Google+ members in this Community. If this looks like something you would be interested in joining, you can do that by clicking on the red button in the upper-right corner of the window labeled "Join Community". When you do that, this Community will show up in your Circles. Anybody can read stuff posted to Public Communities, but if you want to comment or add to the discussion, you have to join.

Figure 12.22 - Clicking on a Community Opens a Page Where You Can Join that Community

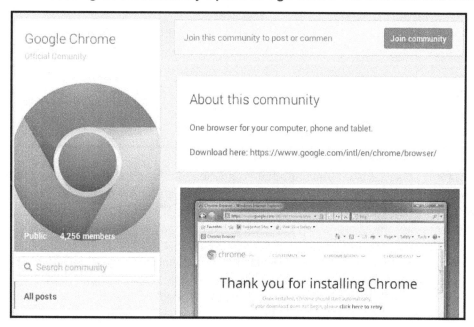

Most Google+ Communities are Public - anyone can view what's posted or join. Some Public Communities are moderated and require you to ask permission from the moderator in order to join.

There are also Private Google+ Communities. These are not visible to the public. Basically you have to know who created the Private Community so that you can ask to join, or you have to be invited to join. I'll discuss this a little further in the next section.

12.5.5   Creating Your Own Google+ Community

If you have searched through all of the available Google+ Communities and still can't find exactly what you are looking for, then you can create a new Community that you and other people can join. Referring back to Figure 12.21, you will see in the upper-right corner of the window a blue button labeled "Create Community". Clicking that button will start the Community creation process by opening a window as illustrated in Figure 12.23.

Figure 12.23 - Clicking on "Create Community" Opens a Page Where You Can Select the Type of Community You Want to Create

A "Public" Community is visible to anyone, that is, anyone can read the Community discussion. But, you may need permission to join the Community so that you can contribute to the discussion. If this is the type of Community you want to create, then select the "Public" type, give your Community a name, and select either the "Anyone can join" or "Anyone can ask to join" menu items.

A "Private" Community can be completely invisible to searches, or it can be findable by doing an appropriate Google search. But nobody can join a Private Community or view posts to that Community unless they get permission from the owner of the Community - that is the person who created it. For example, there may be a group of old buddies who want to get together and talk about "the good old days". They might create a Private Community and make it invisible to search engines. Since they already know everybody that they want to include in the Community, there is no need to expose the Community to public view.

Note: Once a Community is created as either Public or Private, that cannot be changed.

12.5.6 Add to Your Google+ "Following" Circle

Google+ "Communities", which are discussed in the previous section, are like forums where members carry on conversations amongst themselves. There is another type of Google+ group that is more like an rss feed or a blog where a single individual or small group create all the posts and their "followers" simply read or comment on what they write or share. Google describes this type of group as "people you don't know personally, but whose posts you find interesting". Google+ provides an easy way for you to "Discover" these interesting people. Back on your "People" page (Home Page -> People) you will find a Discover" tab. Clicking on this "Discover" tab will open a page where you can indeed discover interesting people and topics. This is illustrated in Figure 12.24.

Figure 12.24 - Selecting the "Discover" Tab on Your "People" Page Opens this Page

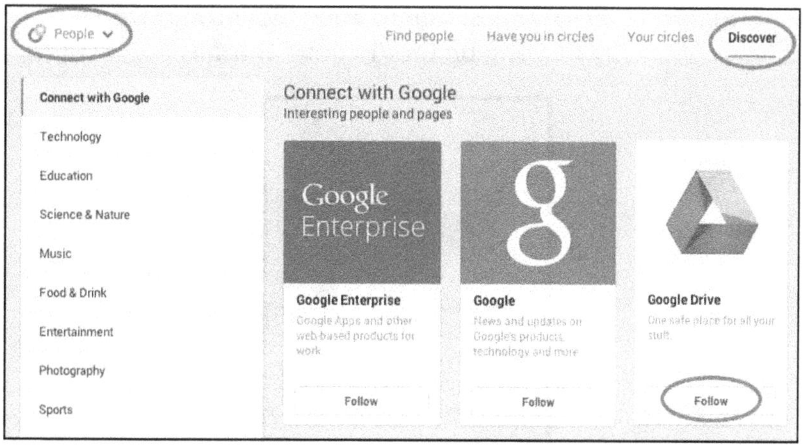

In the left sidebar shown in Figure 12.24 is a list of top level topics that will help you narrow your search for interesting stuff. In this example, I have selected the first item in the menu of topics, "Connect with Google", and that has opened a page, part of which is illustrated in the figure. You will see dozens of topics you can Follow if you choose. In order to get a feel for what a topic contains, just click on the panel for that topic - on the panel not on the "Follow" button. In Figure 12.25 I have clicked on the "Goggle Drive" panel in Figure 12.24.

Figure 12.25 - You Can Read Recent Posts to a Topic Before Deciding to "Follow" It

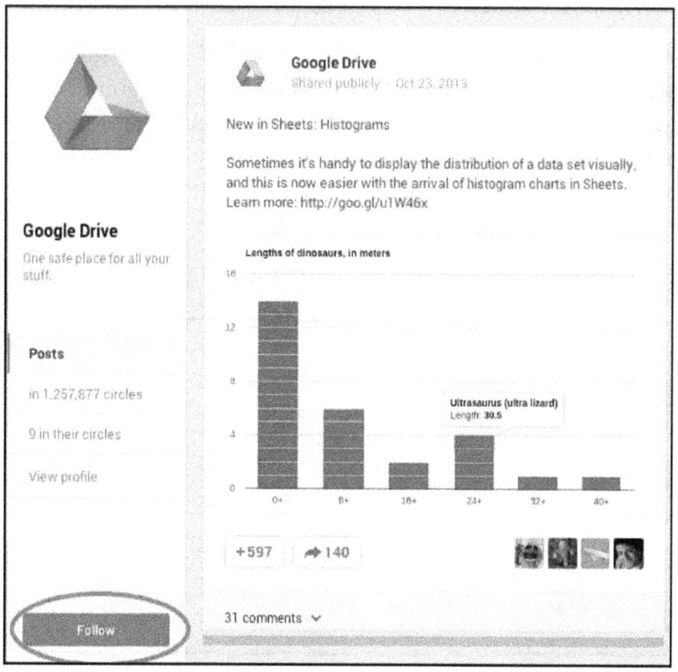

On the page illustrated in Figure 12.25 you can read some recent posts to this topic. If you would like to "Follow" future posts to this topic, just click on the "Follow" button shown outlined in either Figure 12.24 or 12.25. Clicking on "Follow" in either of these pages will open a list of your Circles so that you can choose which Circle to add this topic too. "Following" is the default Circle. This is illustrated in Figure 12.26.

**Figure 12.26 - You Can Add to Your "Following" Circle
by Clicking on the "Follow" Button**

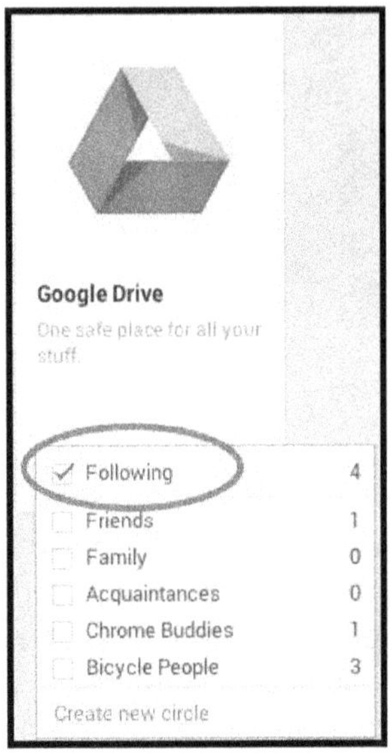

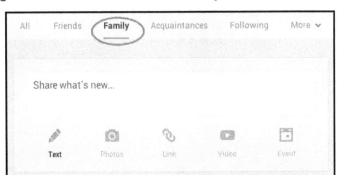

12.6 - Sharing Stuff with Your Google+ Circles

Once you have created and populated your Circles, you can share stuff with the people in those Circles. It's pretty easy. Open your Google+ Home Page (see Section 12.4 if your don't remember how to do this). The top portion of the Google+ Home Page is illustrated in Figure 12.27. Along the top of the Home Page is a row of tabs listing the names of your Circles, "All", "Friends", "Family", etc. In Figure 12.27 Clicking on "More" at the right end of the tab bar will drop-down a menu listing the rest of your Circles. I have selected the "Family" Circle to share with.

Figure 12.27 - You Can Share with Any or All of Your Circles

12.6.1 Sharing Text with Your Selected Circle

At this point you have selected which Circle you want to share with. Now you need to tell Google+ what you want to share. Along the bottom of Figure 12.27 is a row of icons representing the types of things you can share: Text (selected by default), Photos, Links, Videos, or Events. Figure 12.28 shows an example of sharing text. I simply clicked in the "Share what's new ..." box shown in Figure 12.27 and typed in my message.

Figure 12.28 - An Example of Sharing "Text"

At the bottom of Figure 12.28 is an outlined checkbox labeled "Also send email to Family". When you check this box a copy of your message is sent to everyone in the selected Circle by email as well as to their Google+ Home Page. When the recipients in your selected Circle receive your Post on their Google+ Home Page it will look like what is illustrated in Figure 12.29. Notice that they don't actually see your Post, but rather the blue button labeled "1 New" that is outlined in the figure. When they click on this button, your Post will open for them to read.

Figure 12.29 - This is What the Recipient of Your Shared "Post" Will See

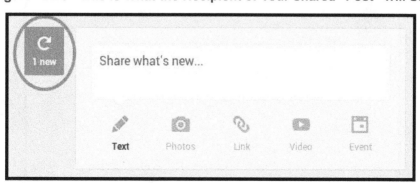

Figure 12.30 - The Recipient of a Post Can Stop Any Future Posts from This Sender

Figure 12.30 is an example of a Post I received in response to my Post to my "Family" Circle. So, in this figure I am the recipient. Near the upper-right corner of received Posts is a downward pointing disclosure triangle which is hidden in Figure 12.30 by the outlined menu box that opened when I clicked on the triangle. This menu offers the recipient of a Post the option to "Mute post". Clicking on this option will prevent the sender from sending any more Posts to this recipient. If someone is sending annoying Posts to you, clicking on "Mute Post" will stop that from happening in the future. In a more severe case you might choose to "Remove from Circles" to remove the sender from all of your Circles. This will prevent any future communication from or to this sender. You can also report this sender as "Spam or Abuse" and Google will handle that situation for you. Back in Section 12.5.3 I said that you cannot stop someone from adding you to their Circles, but you can block communication from them. This is how that is done.

12.6.2 Sharing "Photos", "Links", or "Videos" with Your Selected Circle

As illustrated in Figure 12.28, you can attach photos, links, or videos to a text Post. These work pretty much the same as attaching stuff to an email message. Figure 12.31 shows an example of a text message with an attached Link. To create this Post I went to the web page whose link I wanted to send and copied the link address. I then pasted that link address into the Post I was creating. Figure 12.31 illustrates what the recipient receives when you share a Link.

Figure 12.31 - Example of a Shared Link - This is What the Recipient Sees

Things work in exactly the same way if you click on "Photos", "Links", or "Video" in Figure 12.27 to start your Post. You can still enter text as illustrated in Figure 12.28.

12.6.3 Sharing an "Event" with Your Selected Circle

Sharing "Events" on Google+ is a little different in that you create the Event as part of your Post. Figure 12.32 illustrates the Event creation page that opens when you click on "Event" near the lower-right corner in Figure 12.27 or 12.29.

Figure 12.32 - Creating an "Event" to Share with Your Google+ Circles

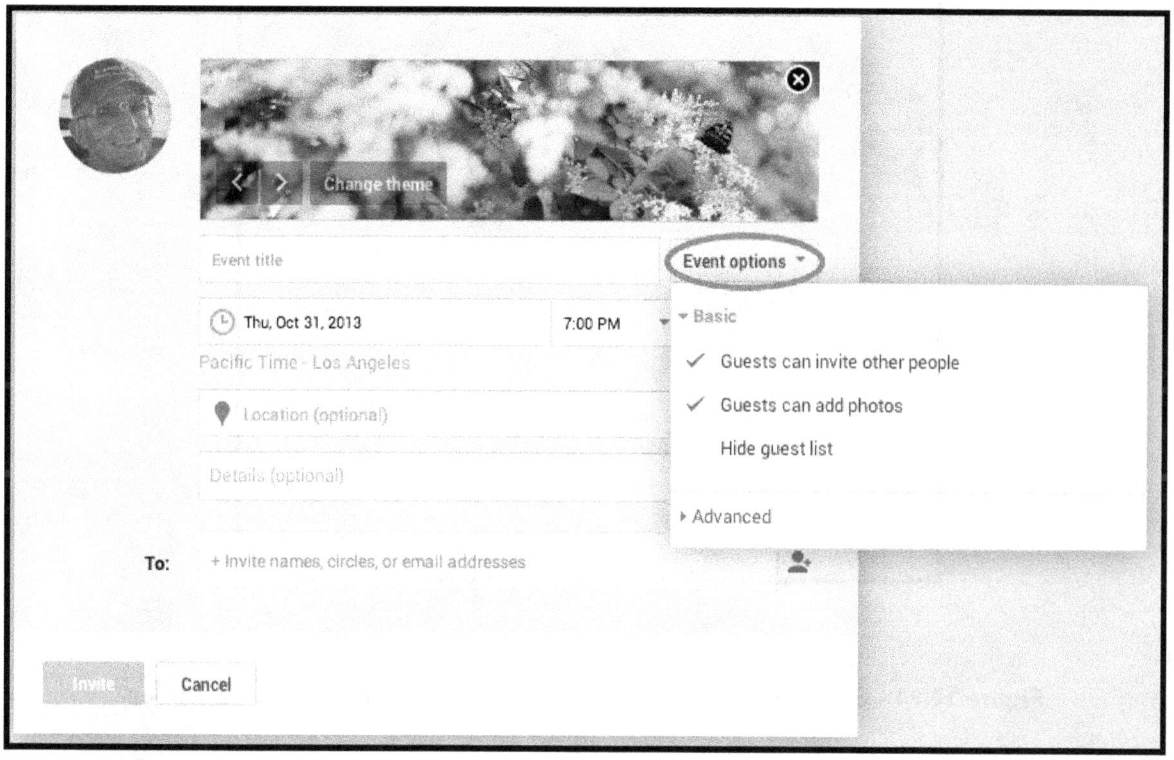

You can change the photo that acts as a "theme" for your Event - a picture of a butterfly and flowers in Figure 12.32. You give your Event a title, a start time and, optionally, an end time (which is hidden in the figure), a location, and other details. You can also select "Event options" as shown in the figure. Once you have filled in all of the information about your Event you can "Invite" people by Circle, or by email address if you want to invite someone who does not have a Google+ Profile.

I created an Event to celebrate publication of my new book (I wish) and sent it to my "Family" Circle. Figure 12.33 on the next page shows what they receive. Each invitee can reply by answering the question "Are You Going?" with "Yes", "Maybe", or "No". If you have permitted it in Figure 12.32 your recipients can send invitations to other people.

When you create an "Event" Post, it gets added to your and to all of your invitees Google Calendars. Figure 12.34 illustrates this. Clicking on the Event in the Google Calendar (outlined in the figure) opens the invitation as illustrated. Your invitees can reply directly in this Calendar view.

Figure 12.33 - Example of a Shared Event - This is What the Recipient Sees on Their Google+ Home Page

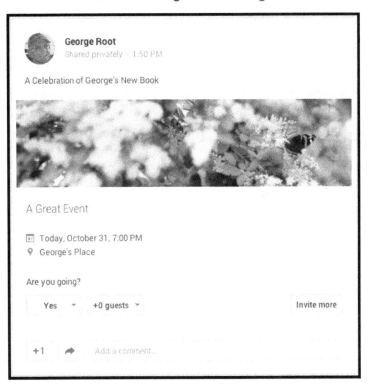

Figure 12.34 - Example of a Shared Event - This is What the Recipient Sees in Their Google Calendar

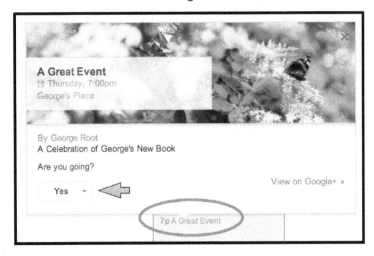

12.7 - Google+ "Hangouts"

Before we start, let me say that Google Hangouts is a relatively new service and things are changing fairly rapidly. So, when you read this, things may not look nor operate exactly as I will be describing. Hopefully the following will give you enough information to get started even if some things have changed since I wrote this.

Google "Hangouts" is a service that allows you to hold a "conversation" with friends, family, and other people in your Google+ Circles. Although you can "Hangout" with people who are not Google+ members, all participants need to have Google+ Profiles in order to have access to all of Hangouts features such as making group video calls, sharing photos, and connecting with Google+ Circles.

You can hold a "Hangout" in one of three forms:

1) You can exchange text messages, photos and "emoji" symbols with up to 100 people. Hangouts has about 800 emoji symbols available. Here are a few:

2) You can take part in a Video conference call among up to 10 people. You need to have a broadband internet connection to make video Hangouts.

3) You can participate in a "Hangouts on the Air" broadcast.

I will introduce each of these in following sections. But first we need to install the various Hangouts extensions and apps.

12.7.1 Installing the Hangouts Extensions and Apps

Google Hangouts runs on all of your devices. But, before you can use Hangouts on all these devices, you need to install the necessary extensions and apps. Once you do this, your Hangouts remain synchronized on all devices. You can start a Hangout on one device and finish it on another.

Installing "Hangouts" as an Extension to the Chrome Browser or Chrome OS:

The Hangouts extension for the Chrome web browser or the Chrome OS is available free from the Chrome Web Store (see Section 2.7 in the original volume). Just go to the store and search for "Hangouts".

https://chrome.google.com/webstore

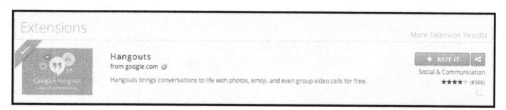

Installing the "Hangouts" App on Your iPhone or iPad:

The iPhone or iPad Hangouts app is available free on the iTunes App Store. You can download the Google+ app at the same time if you have not done that already.

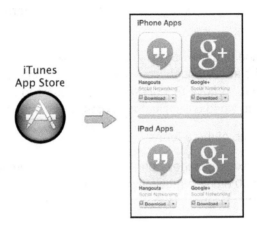

Installing the "Hangouts" App on Your Android Device:

The Android Hangouts app is available free at the Google Play Web Store. Just go to the Google Play store (see Section 2.7 in the original volume) and search for "Hangouts".

https://chrome.google.com/webstore/search/hangouts?hl=en

12.7.1   "Hanging Out" via Text Messages

With Hangouts you can send messages, photos, and emoji symbols to friends, family, and other people in your Circles. You can start a Hangout using the Hangouts extension to the Chrome web browser or OS, or with the Hangouts app on your mobile device. Just look for the green Hangouts icon which is illustrated in the figure just above. On your mobile device, you will launch the Hangouts app identified with this icon. With the Chrome web browser or OS you will find the Hangouts extension icon in your row of extensions as illustrated in Figure 12.35 on the next page.

Figure 12.35 - The Hangouts Extension Icon is in the Row of Extensions at the Top of the Chrome Browser Window.

Clicking on the Hangouts icon will open a small window, probably designed for a smartphone, where you can choose whom to hangout with. The top portion of this window is shown in Figure 12.36. Click in the "+ New Hangout" area to start the process.

Figure 12.36 - The Top Portion of the Hangouts Window is Where You Choose the People You Want to Hangout With

Once you click on "+ New Hangout", Google will suggest a list of people you might want to Hangout with. If the person you want is on the list, just click on the square box next to the person's name shown outlined in Figure 12.37. If the person or Circle you want is not in the suggested list, you can enter the name, email address, phone number, or the name of a Circle with which to start a Hangout. If you enter a person's name, you will get a long list of people with that name who have Google+ accounts from which you can choose the right person. Entering a phone number, to connect with someone using their mobile phone, will only work if the person has given their correct phone number when they signed up for Hangouts. In the example illustrated in Figure 12.37, I have typed the name "Family" and Hangouts has suggested my Family Circle. Once Hangouts has correctly identified the person or Circle you are trying to connect with, click on the little square box next to their name which is shown outlined in the figure.

Figure 12.37 - Click the Square Box Next to the Correct Name

Clicking on the box outlined in Figure 12.37 will add that person or Circle to your Hangout. It will also change the Hangouts window to be as illustrated in Figure 12.38. Although it is not apparent in this figure, there is a text insertion point just below the name "Family" that has already been added to the Hangout. This allows you to type in an identifier for someone else that you would like to add. Just follow the same process described above to add as many people as you like to your Hangout. You can have a text message Hangout with as many as 100 people or a video call Hangout with up to 10 people.

Figure 12.38 - You Can Add More People or Circles to Your Hangout

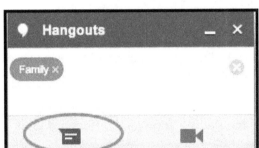

If you try to initiate a Hangout with someone who doesn't have Hangouts installed, a message will be sent to their email address inviting them to join Hangouts.

If you try to initiate a Hangout with someone who has Hangouts installed but who is not signed-in at this time, they will receive a notification that they can join your Hangout the next time they sign-in to Hangouts. You will also receive a message at the bottom of the Hangouts window telling you that they are not available right now and that they will receive a Notification when they sign-in. If you are not in one of their Circles they will receive a Hangouts request from you.

OK, now that you have filled out the list of people and Circles you want to Hangout with, you need to decide whether you want to hold a text message Hangout or a video conference call Hangout. Both are free. In the example illustrated in Figure 12.38, I have outlined the button used to start a text message Hangout. Clicking on this button will send out your invitations to Hangout to all of the people or Circles you have listed.

Figure 12.39 - Type Your Message and Hit "Return"
Your Message Will Be Sent to Everyone in the Hangout

As the title of Figure 12.39 says, all you have to do is type your message and hit "Return" or "Enter" and your message will be sent to everyone in your Hangout. I have typed in "Hi - Are you at home?" as an example in Figure 12.39.

Figure 12.40 - Type Your Message and Hit "Return"

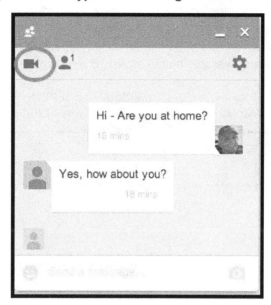

Figure 12.40 is an example of how the conversation progresses. Each time someone sends a message, it appears at the bottom of the list of messages with the sender's photo next to it.

To insert an emoji symbol into your message, click on the faint emoji face show at the bottom-left corner of Figure 12.39. This will open a menu of items that you can choose from as illustrated in Figure 12.41. Click on your desired emoji from this menu and it will be inserted into your message.

Figure 12.41 - You Can Insert Emoji Symbols into Your Messages

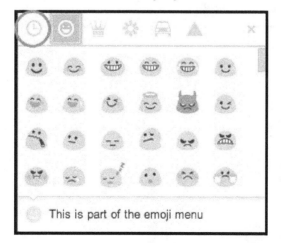

The "clock" icon circled in the upper-left corner of Figure 12.41 reveals a list of your recently used emoji when it is clicked. So, it is really a "Recently Used Emoji" button and not a clock.

12.7.2 "Hanging Out" via Video Conference Calls

As discussed in the previous section, you can Hangout with a group of friends by exchanging text messages. With Hangouts you can also hold video Hangouts with up to 9 other people. You initiate a video Hangout by clicking on the video camera icon shown circled in the upper-left corner of Figure 12.40 or in the lower-right corner of Figure 12.38. As Figure 12.40 illustrates, you can start with a text message Hangout and then switch to a video conference. This might be a good idea if your want to be sure that the other people are available before starting the video.

**Figure 12.42 - The First Time You Start a Video Hangout
You May Have to Install a Browser Plugin**

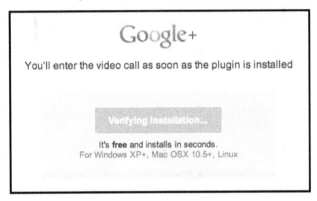

Once any necessary plugins have been installed, the video conference will be started. Your recipients, who have Hangouts running, will hear a pleasing ringtone letting them know that someone is trying to connect with them on a video Hangout. The video window will look something like that illustrated in Figure 12.43. Your picture will be in the lower-right corner of your screen and the picture of the person you are Hanging Out with will be in the big blank area of Figure 12.43.

Figure 12.43 - This is a Simplified Illustration of the Video Hangout Window

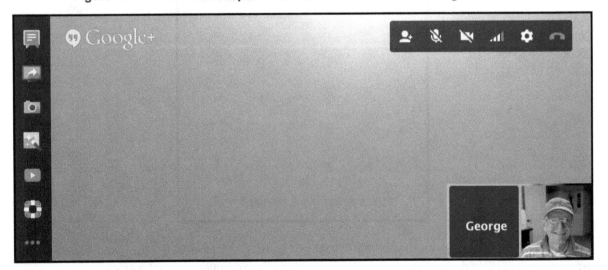

If you move your cursor inside the video window, the two toolbars shown in Figure 12.43 will appear. The top toolbar buttons do these things:

- The "person+" button at the left end of the toolbar allows you to add people to the video conference.

- The "microphone" button turns off your microphone so that the other people can't hear what you are saying.

- The "video camera" button turns off your video camera so that the other people can't see you.

- The "4-bar" button that looks like a cell phone signal strength meter allows you to adjust the quality of your video signal so as to change the data bandwidth needed.

- The "gear" button appears to simply list your video input and your audio input and output devices. I'm not sure what this accomplishes. Perhaps it will allow you to change devices sometime in a future upgrade.

- And finally, the "red phone" button allows you to hangup - that is to disconnect from the video conference.

The buttons in the vertical toolbar at the left edge of the video window do these things:

Figure 12.44 - Labels for the Buttons in the Vertical Toolbar

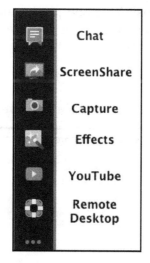

- The "Chat" button starts a separate text message chat session

- The "Screen Share" button will ask if you want to share your screen with the other members of your Hangout. If you say "Yes", you will be presented with a thumbnail view of all the open windows on your screen. You select one and that window is shared with your conferees. It replaces your video feed. This might be useful if you were discussing something on your screen, say a diagram, and wanted everyone to be able to see what you were talking about.

- The "Capture" button captures a screen shot of your video feed and shares that photo with all members of the video chat session.

- The "Effects" button lets you add various "special effects" to your video feed. These include various sound effects, various articles of head ware that you can hover over your face in your video feed and lots of other stuff you might like to explore.

- The "YouTube" button opens a YouTube feed that you can share with your Hangout participants.

- The "Remote Desktop" button is, according to Google, "A Hangouts app for people to help other people with their computers by controlling them remotely (with their permission, of course)". This sounds like a recipe for disaster, but your mileage may vary.

When you are done with your video chat session, just click on the "Red Phone" button at the right end of the top toolbar shown in Figure 12.43.

12.7.3 Placing Phone Calls Using Hangouts

In addition to video conference calls, you can also make regular voice calls to any phone number. Calls to the US and Canada are free. To make calls to other countries, you have to sign up for a Google Wallet account in order to buy calling credits. You can start the sign-up process by going here:

http://www.google.com/wallet/

Google Wallet can also be used to pay for online purchases if the vendor allows Google Wallet payments. The advantage of paying this way is that your credit card information is not sent to the vendor. This works pretty much like PayPal.

The cost to call a few countries is shown in Figure 12.45:

Figure 12.45 - Some Representative Overseas Calling Costs

See how our super low rates compare to the competition:	
Country	Google Voice rate per minute
France - Mobile	10¢
Germany - Mobile	10¢
India - Mobile	2¢
Mexico - Mobile	15¢
United States	☆ free from the U.S. & Canada 1¢ from everywhere else

OK, placing a phone call is pretty simple:

1) Click on the Hangouts app icon to open a new Hangouts window as illustrated in Figure 12.46

2) Click on the drop-down menu icon near the upper-right corner of the window (it looks like a downward pointing triangle as shown in Figure 12.46)

3) Click on "Call a Phone", shown outlined in Figure 12.46, This will open a window where you can enter the number of the phone you want to call. If the person you are calling is in your Contacts Book, you can select their number from the list that appears.

Figure 12.46 - Start the Calling Process by Clicking on "Call a Phone"

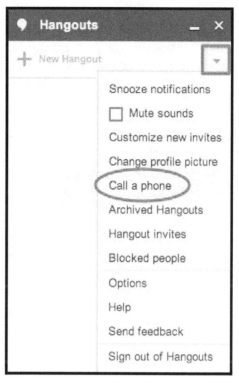

4) If you know the country code for the country you are calling, you can type it in as part of the phone number. If you don't know the country code, clicking on the disclosure triangle next to the American flag as shown in Figure 12.47 will drop down a list of countries and their codes. Just click on the one you want. Calling to a US phone is the default and if this is the country you want, you don't have to worry about country codes.

Figure 12.47 - You Can Select a Country Code from the Drop-Down Menu

5) Then just fill in the rest of the number you want to call and hit "Return"

12.7.4 "Hangouts on the Air"

A Google "Hangout on the Air" is actually a video conference call that is converted into a YouTube video that is then broadcast in real time. Anybody can watch the participants talking with one another and answering questions from the "audience". Hangouts-on-the-Air are scheduled Events. You can watch one that is going on right now, or you can tune in to a future Hangout-on-the-Air at its scheduled time.

Watching a Hangout-on-the-Air that is In-Progress

To start watching a Hangout-on-the-Air that has already started, hover your cursor over the "Home" icon on any Google+ page to reveal the Google+ menu and then select "Hangouts-on-the-Air" as illustrated in Figure 12.48.

Figure 12.48 - You Can Start Watching an "On-the-Air" Hangout by Selecting "Hangouts on Air" from the Google+ Menu

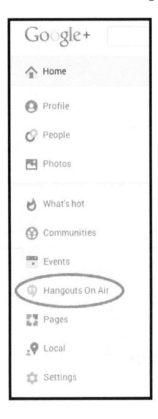

This will open a window showing a large number of Hangout-on-the-Air that are taking place right now. A portion of the page showing Hangouts-on-the-Air that are being broadcast as I'm writing this is shown in Figure 12.49. Some are more interesting than others. If you want to see what's going on, just click on the "Play" button in the center of each video.

Figure 12.49 - You Can Watch a Live Hangouts-on-the-Air in Progress

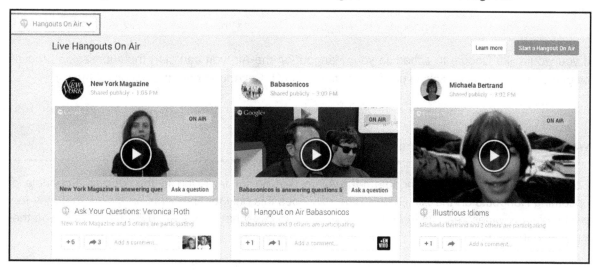

Start Your Own **Hangout-on-the-Air**

If you think that you have something to say that other people might find interesting, you can create your own Hangout-on-the-Air. To get started, click on the "Start a Hangout-on-the-Air" button in the upper-right corner of Figure 12.49. This will open a dialog as illustrated in Figure 12.50.

Figure 12.50 - To Create Your Own Hangout-on-the-Air
You Must Link Your Google+ Account to a YouTube Account

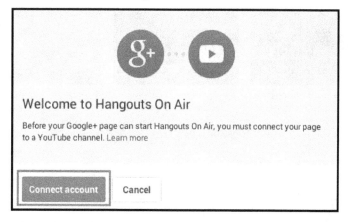

As the dialog says, you have to connect your Google+ account with a YouTube account. The process for doing this is somewhat involved, so to save space, I am just going to point you toward a page that will explain the process:

https://support.google.com/youtube/topic/3024170?hl=en-GB&ref_topic=3024169

You can also find answers to common questions about creating your own Hangout-on-the-Air at this site:

https://support.google.com/plus/answer/2459411?hl=en&ref_topic=2553242

If you would like Google to schedule your Hangout-on-the-Air, you can start the submission process by going to this site and clicking on "Hangouts-on-the-Air Schedule" near the bottom of the list.

https://support.google.com/plus/answer/3136020?hl=en

Watching a Scheduled Hangout-on-the-Air

Some people submit their Hangout-on-the-Air to Google for inclusion in the "official" Schedule of upcoming Hangouts-on-the-Air. Google generally does this only for Hangouts-on-the-Air that they feel will be of fairly widespread interest. If you would like to see what's coming up in the Hangouts-on-the-Air Schedule, go to this site:

http://www.google.com/intl/en/+/learnmore/hangouts/schedule.html

where you will find a list of upcoming Scheduled Hangouts-on-the-Air. An example of a portion of the page that opens is illustrated in Figure 12.51. Those shown in the figure will have already happened by the time you read this. But there will be dozens of upcoming Scheduled Hangouts on the page that you see.

Figure 12.51 - An Example of a Few Scheduled Google+ Hangouts-on-the-Air

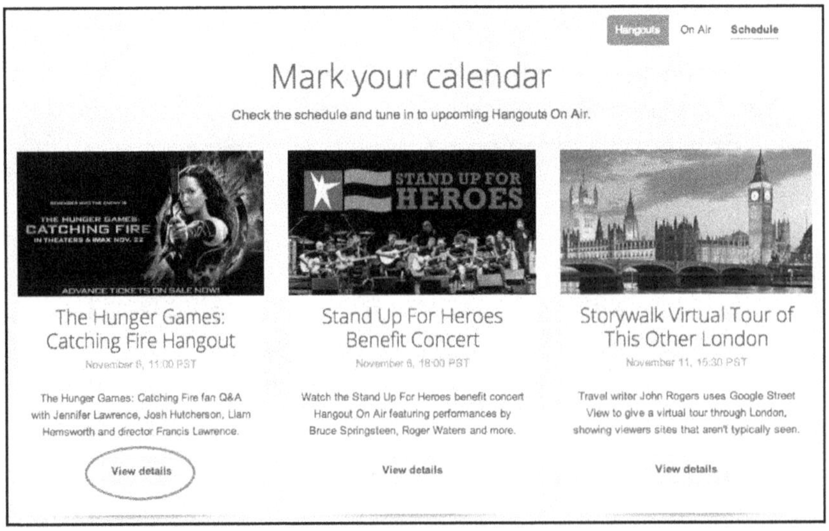

As you can see, in order for Google to Schedule your Hangout, it has to be "serious" and of general interest. Don't bother to submit a Hangout of you playing with your cat.

Clicking on the "View Details" button shown outlined in Figure 12.51 will open a page similar to that illustrated in Figure 12.52 on the next page.

Figure 12.52 - An Example of the Details Page for a Scheduled Google+ Hangout-on-the-Air

Clicking on the scheduled time of the Hangout-on-the-Air will create an Event in your Google Calendar. You can also read more details about the Hangout-on-the-Air. Viewers can ask questions during the live broadcast. When the broadcast is finished, it will be saved as a YouTube video, so you can see these events even if you miss the Scheduled live broadcast.

12.7.5   Google+ Settings

As I said at the beginning of this section, Google+ is huge! I have only touched on a few details about some of the more interesting portions of Google+. There is a lot more for you to explore. One final topic that you should look into is Google+ Settings where you will be able to set controls on how Google+ works for you. For example, you can turn "Notifications" ON or OFF for dozens of different events that might trigger a Notification to you. If you become overwhelmed by being constantly "Notified" of Google+ related events, you can turn them off for each different type of event.

To get to your Google+ Settings page, just hover your cursor over the "Home" icon on your Google+ Home Page and select "Settings" which will be the last item in the drop-down menu. You can see this in Figure 12.48.

13 - Editing Your Photos

Taking and sharing photos is an important part of the social networking experience and Google has made that easy, particularly as a part of Google+ which I discussed in the previous section.

13.1 - Taking and Editing Photos on Your Mobile Device

If you take a photo using your mobile phone or tablet, you can do some minimal editing right on your mobile device before sharing it with friends. The "Camera" apps on mobile devices have some minimal built-in editing capability and you could use these native camera apps and the editing features they provide. Or, you can take your photos using the Google+ app on your mobile device. Google+ uses the same camera, but it connects your photos directly to your Google+ Account. Google+ offers an "Auto Backup" feature that automatically uploads your photos, as you take them, to your Goggle+ photo album. This is very handy if you use Google+ to share stuff.

If you would like to have your photos automatically backed up to Google+, you have to enable that on your mobile device. The first time you run the Google+ app on your mobile device, you should be asked if you want to turn Auto-Backup ON. Just answer "Yes" and allow Google+ to access your photos and you're set to go. If you skipped this step during your first-run, you can turn auto-backup ON or OFF by following these steps:

13.1.1 Enable Google+ Auto-Backup On iOS Devices

With the Google+ app running on your iOS device:
- Go to your Google+ Home screen
- Touch the Google+ Menu icon (three horizontal bars in the upper-left corner)
- Touch the "Gear" icon in the upper-right corner
- Touch "Camera and Photos"
- Toggle the On/Off switch to ON.
- You can also select some backup options. For example, you might want to perform backups only when you are connected to a Wi-Fi network.

13.1.2 Enable Google+ Auto-Backup On Android Devices

With the Google+ app running on your Android device:
- Go to your Goole+ Home screen
- Touch the Google+ Menu icon
- Touch "Settings"
- Touch "Auto Backup"
- Toggle the On/Off switch to ON.
- You can also select some backup options. For example, you might want to perform backups only when you are connected to a Wi-Fi network.

13.1.3 Editing Photos Using Google+ on Your Mobile Device

If you take photos on your mobile device using the Google+ app, instead of the device's built-in "Camera" app, you can edit the photos and share them with friends and Google+ Circles right from your mobile device.

To edit your photos taken using the Google+ app (these illustrations are from Google+ running on an iPhone):

1) Go to your Google+ Home Screen and touch the "Photos" menu item

2) You will see a set of photo albums labeled by date. Select one of these albums and then a photo from that album.

3) Touch the "Gear" icon in the upper-right corner of the screen. This will drop down a menu as illustrated in Figure 13.1.

Figure 13.1 - Select a Photo, Touch the Gear Icon, and then Select "Edit"

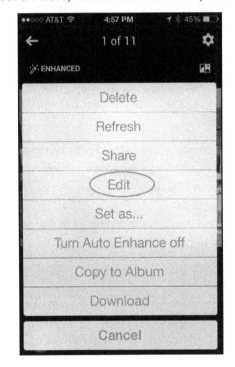

4) Touch "Edit" shown outlined in Figure 13.1. This will open the editing window as illustrated in Figure 13.2 on the next page. The four types of editing provided by the mobile version of Google+ are: Auto Enhance, Rotate, Crop, and Filters. Touching "Filters" also allows you to select a frame for your photo.

"Auto Enhance" appears to be an all-or-nothing feature. Your photo is "Enhanced" or it is not. You can turn "Enhance" OFF or ON using the menu illustrated in Figure 13.1. The button for this is just two steps below the "Edit" button.

Figure 13.2 - The Mobile Google+ Edit Screen Offers Four Types of Edits

"Crop" and "Rotate" are pretty self-explanatory. The "Filters" editing option allows you to vary the color and style of your photo. There are 9 basic filter types and many of these have multiple versions. This is illustrated in Figure 13.3.

Figure 13.3 - There are Several Types of "Filters" Available

In Figure 13.3 I have selected the "Drama 1" filter by touching it. When you touch one of the Filter type buttons, that button gets outlined with a blue square outline as shown in the figure. It is difficult to see in the figure, but near the bottom of the square outline around "Drama 1" there are two very faint dots. Easier to see, there is a "Circulating Arrows" icon in the center of the box. These two items, the dots and circulating arrows, indicate that there are variations on the "Drama 1" Filter. To see the other style variations, just tap the Filter button that you have selected, "Drama 1" in this example. With each tap a different style variation will be applied to your photo. If you continue tapping, the style variations will cycle around and around. Stop tapping when you find a style that you like.

There is a second item to take notice of in Figure 13.3. The small letter "I" inside a small white circle near the upper-left corner of the Edit window does not reveal information about your photo as you might expect. Instead, touching this "i" icon reveals the informative panel shown in Figure 13.4.

Figure 13.4 - Tapping the "i" Reveals this Information

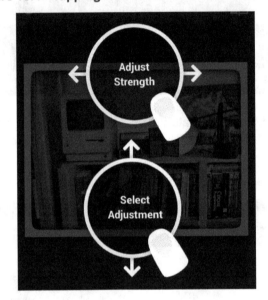

There are two messages in this panel:

1) Touching the screen and sliding your finger up or down reveals a short menu that allows you to select a type of adjustment that you can apply to this Filter. For example, with the "Drama 1" Filter selected, moving my finger up and down the screen allows me to select "Saturation" or "Style Strength" as a type of adjustment I can apply to the "Drama 1" Filter.

2) Once you have selected the type of adjustment you want, moving your finger sideways allows you to adjust the strength of the adjustment.

There is a third item to take notice of in Figure 13.3. The squarish button in the upper-right corner of the screen allows you to compare the edited version of your photo with the original, unedited, version. Touch this button and the unedited version will appear. Un-touch this button and the edited version will appear.

Once you have your photo edited to your satisfaction, touching the check-mark icon in the lower-right corner will apply your edits and save this edited version of your photo. If you get hopelessly lost in all this and just want to start over, touching the "X" in the lower-left corner of the screen will cancel all of your edits and return you to the photo chooser screen.

13.2 - Editing Photos on Your Chromebook or in the Chrome Browser

If you have Chrome version 30 or later, the capabilities of the SnapSeed photo editor are built in. But, before you can edit your photos, you have to get them into Google+. You can import photos from your mobile device, or from a stand-alone camera.

13.2.1 Uploading Photos from Your Mobile Device to Google+

Uploading photos from your mobile device was described in Section 13.1. Basically, all you have to do is enable "Automatic Backups" and any photos you take using the camera in your mobile device will be uploaded to the Google+ servers.

13.2.2 Uploading Photos from Your Camera to Google+

You can connect your stand-alone camera to your computer using a USB cable, but I find that the easiest way to upload photos from my camera is simply to remove the SD memory card from the camera and insert it into the SD card slot on my Chromebook or on my Mac.

One way to transfer photos to Google+ is first to transfer them into your Google Drive folder. On a Chromebook, you will use the Chrome "Files" app to do this. This is discussed in Sections 2.4.1 and 4.5 of the original volume. First create a folder in your Google Drive to receive the photos and then drag the selected photos from the SD card into this Google Drive folder. Once you have your photos stored in your Google Drive, there is a Google+ Setting that allows you to view photos stored in your Google Drive from within Google+ (only JPEG, GIF, WebP, and RAW files can be viewed this way).

The first time you launch Google+ after putting photos into your Google Drive folder, you should be presented with a panel as illustrated in Figure 13.5

Figure 13.5 - Enable "Show Drive Photos in Google+"

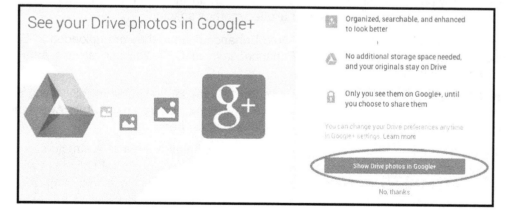

If you don't see this panel, you can go to the Google+ Settings page and enable Google Drive photos there. To open your Google+ Settings go to your Google+ Home Page and select the "Settings" item from the drop-down menu under the "Home" icon. "Settings" should be the last item in the list. Select the "Photos" settings page. This is illustrated in Figure 13.6. Check the Google Drive item as shown.

Figure 13.6 - You Can Enable Google Drive Photo Viewing in Your Google+ Settings

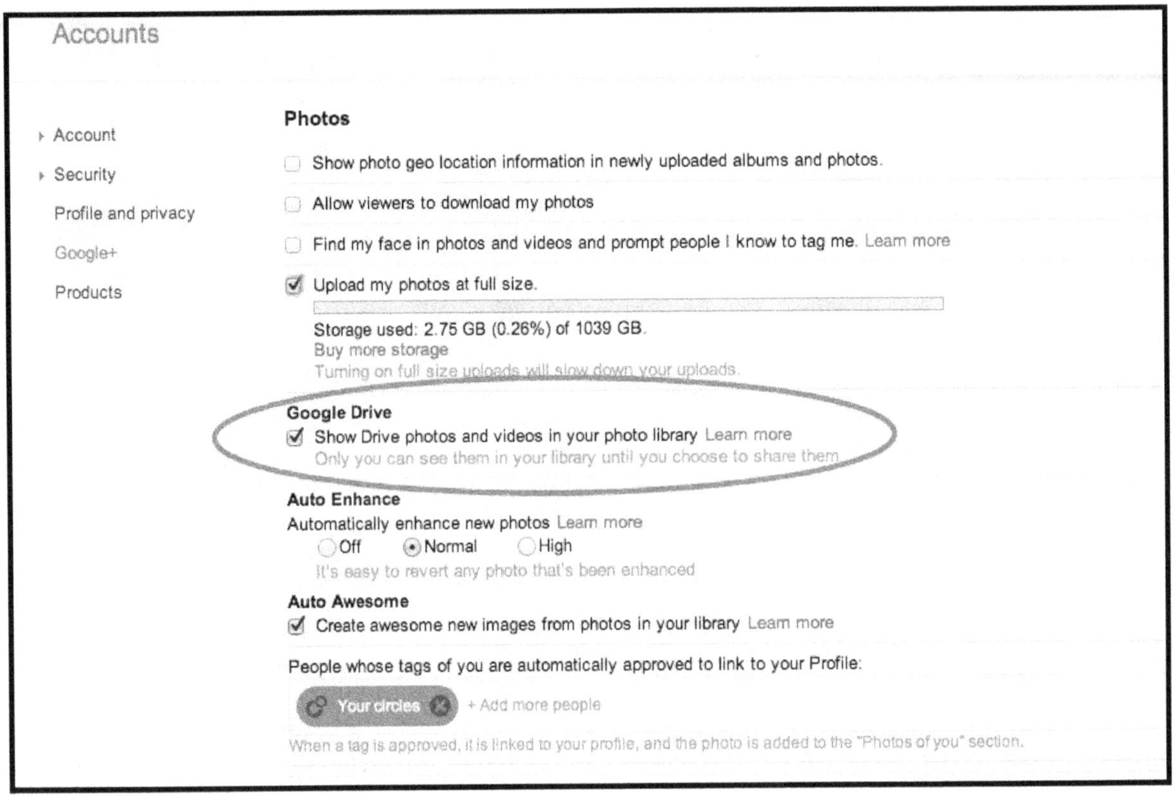

There are a couple of other things you might want to select or de-select in your Google+ Photos settings.

- By default your photos are uploaded to Google+ at a resolution of 2048 pixels on the longest side. If you would rather have them uploaded full size, then you want to check the box labeled "Upload my photos at full size". You can upload an unlimited number of default sized photos, but full size photos count against your allotted storage space.

- By default, all of your photos will be "Auto Enhanced" when they are uploaded to Google+. If you don't want this, set the "Auto Enhance" item to OFF. You can always Auto Enhance individual photos later.

- By default, Google+ will create "Auto Awesome" photos for you automatically. If you don't want this to happen, un-click the "Auto Awesome" checkbox. There are six Auto Awesome effects that Google+ can create. Here's how Google describes them:

    1) **Eraser** - If you take a sequence of 3 or more photos in front of a structure or landmark with movement in the background, Eraser will give you a photo with all the moving objects removed. It's helpful for those situations when you're trying to get a great shot of a landmark or other crowded place, but want to avoid including all of the people in the background of your photo.

    2) **Action** - Take a series of photos of someone moving (dancing, running, jumping) and Auto Awesome will merge them together into one action shot where you can see the full range of movements in a single image, capturing the movement in one captivating still.

3) **Pano** - If you've taken a series of photos with overlapping landscape views, Auto Awesome will stitch these photos together into a panoramic image.

4) **HDR** - High Dynamic Range is the process of taking multiple exposures of the same image. By merging these images together, your photos will achieve a greater range of shadows and light. Uploading three similar images at different exposures--low, medium, and high exposure--will create an HDR image for you.

5) **Motion** - If you've taken a series of photos in succession (at least 5), Auto Awesome will stitch these photos together into a short animation.

6) **Smile** - If you've taken a few group photos, Auto Awesome will choose the best shots of each person in your image and merge them into one great looking photo.

As you can see, some of these effects are what might be expected in a high priced photo editing app but with Google+ you have them free.

13.2.3 Editing Photos in Google+

In order to edit your photos in Google+, you must be using a Chrome OS device or the Chrome Browser on your personal computer. You cannot do this using Safari nor Internet Explorer.

To get started, open your Google+ Home Page and select "Photos" from the menu that drops down when you hover your cursor over the "Home" button in the upper-left corner. This will open a page, a portion of which is shown in Figure 13.7. Click on the "Albums" tab to see the albums you have created in Google+ (there are none in the figure), and any photo folders you have created on your Google Drive. There is one Google Drive folder illustrated in Figure 13.7 - "2013 Pinnacles". In Google Drive, this is a folder, but in Google+ it is treated as an album. You can tell that this is a Google Drive folder because of the very small Drive icon circled in the figure.

Figure 13.7 - Google Drive Folders Containing Photos Show Up as Albums in Google+

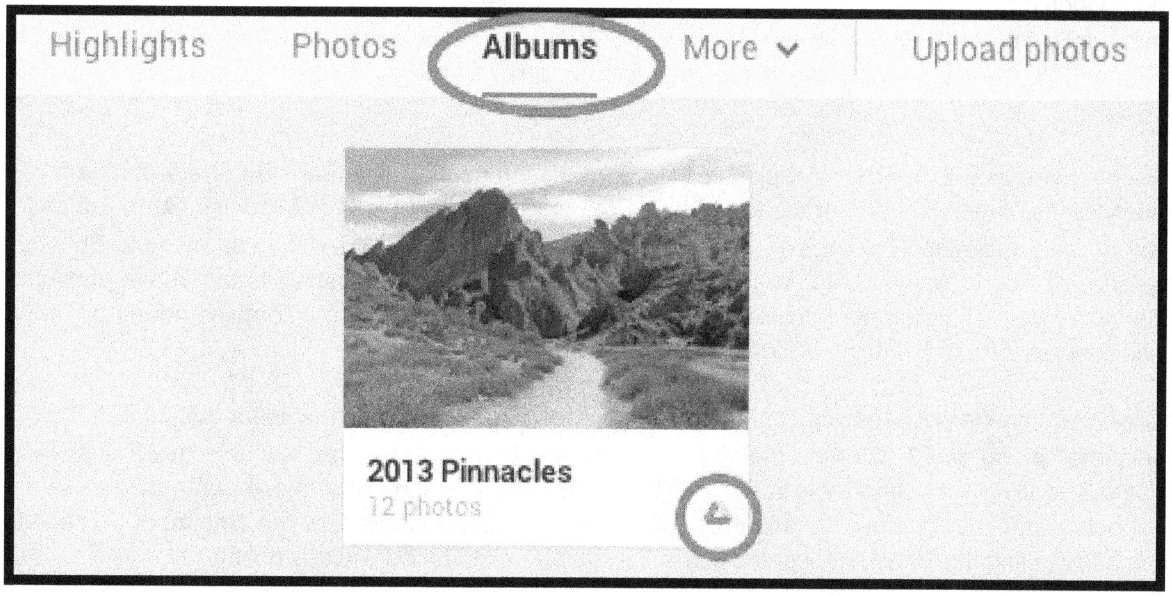

Clicking on the Albums tab in Figure 13.7 allows you to select one album, or in this case one Google Drive folder of photos. Clicking on the album cover photo, such as the one shown in Figure 13.7, will display all of the photos in that album. And finally, clicking on one of these photos will open a page similar to the one illustrated in Figure 13.8 where you will be able to edit that photo.

Figure 13.8 - Clicking on a Photo Opens a Page with that Photo and the Photo's Meta-Data

When you select a photo, that photo opens as illustrated in Figure 13.8 along with a panel that shows, on a Google map, where the photo was taken (if the camera had a GPS), and all of the other photo meta-data: f/number, shutter speed, file size, etc. When you click on the "Edit" tab shown outlined in Figure 13.8, the meta-data panel is replaced with an array of editing controls as illustrated in Figure 13.9.

Each square icon along the right side of Figure 13.9 represents a different type of edit that you can apply to the selected photo. At the top of this array of editing controls is one labeled "Auto-Enhance" with a button labeled "Customize". Clicking on "Auto-Enhance" will apply the current Auto-Enhance settings to the displayed photo. You can change the various photo adjustments that make up "Auto-Enhance" by clicking on the "Customize" button. The Auto-Enhance panel contains nearly all of the adjustments included in the individual controls below it.

Clicking on an individual editing control icon will open a panel with adjustments for that control. This is illustrated in Figure 13.10 where the adjustment panels for the "Tune Image", "Selective Adjust", and "Details" editing controls shown in Figure 13.9 have been opened. All of these controls work in the expected way: moving the sliders to the right or left increases or decreases the amount of that edit to the photo. I find the "Structure" control in the "Details" panel to be particularly useful.

Figure 13.9 - Clicking on a "Edit" Opens a Panel with Editing Controls

Figure 13.10 - Three of the Editing Controls Obtained by Clicking on the Individual Control Icons in Figure 13.9

In Figure 13.10, the center panel labeled "Selective Adjust" deserves special discussion. All of the other editing controls apply their adjustments to the entire photo. "Selective Adjust" allows you to apply a limited number of adjustments to just a limited area of the photo. To do this, you first click on "Add Control Point" -- the circle with the + sign in it in the center panel of Figure 13.10 -- and then click on a point in the photo which will be the center of a circle inside of which the adjustments will be applied. When you click in the photo, it will look something like this -->

The open circle is where I clicked. This will be the center of a circle inside of which the adjustments will be applied. Google+ "feathers" the edges of this adjustment circle so that there will be no abrupt discontinuities in the resulting photo. The top control, the one that looks like a white circle with a double ended arrow inside, allows the size of the adjustment circle in the photo to be changed. I can't show you what this looks like, but all you have to do is click and hold on the double arrow size adjustor and then drag toward or away from the center circle to make the radius of the adjustment circle bigger or smaller. When you are happy with the size, just release the mouse button.

The other three white circles in the figure above represent the controls that can be adjusted. "B" is for Brightness, "C" is for Contrast, and "S" is for Saturation. A somewhat limited set of adjustments, but because they can be applied to just a small area of the photo, they can be quite useful.

13.3 - Other Ways to Edit Your Photos

- **SnapSeed:** SnapSeed is a photo editing app that Google purchased a few years ago and has since incorporated into Google+. All of the photo editing features I have described in the previous section are part of SnapSeed. The SnapSeed app has even more capabilities and is available for iPhone, iPad, and Android devices. Just visit the iTunes app store or the Google Play app store and search for "SnapSeed". It's free.

- **NIK Photo Editing Suite**: SnapSeed is actually a subset of a much more "professional" photo editing suite developed by NIK Software. The whole suite has been purchased by Google and is available for both Mac OS and Windows computers for US$150. A 15 day free trial is available. To read more about it go to:

  http://www.google.com/nikcollection/

- **Pixlr:** Pixlr is a very popular photo editing app. It is also free. It is available for Chrome in the Chrome Web Store. Pixlr Express, a simplified version, is available for iPhone and iPad in the iTunes App Store, and for Android devices in the Google Play Store. Pixlr has one feature that many photo editing apps do not - the ability to distort photos. This is indispensable if you want to correct perspective distortion in your photos caused by a wide field of view and a tilted camera.

  The Chrome Web Store = https://chrome.google.com/webstore/category/apps

  The Google Play Store for Android Devices = https://play.google.com/store/apps

  The iTunes App Store = launch iTunes and click on iTunes Store -> App Store

These two photos are the original version right out of the camera and the version after applying the "Drama" filter in Google+. It is possible to achieve some pretty remarkable results using the free photo editing capabilities built into Google+.

www.ingramcontent.com/pod-product-compliance
Lightning Source LLC
Chambersburg PA
CBHW080429060326
40689CB00019B/4443